MOSTLY

THE^FOOTBALL WORLD ACCORDING TO

OLLIE

THE ^MOSTLY FOOTBALL WORLD ACCORDING TO

OLLIE

IAN HOLLOWAY

Reach Sport

www.reachsport.com

Reach **Sport**

www.reachsport.com

Written with David Clayton.

Published in Great Britain and Ireland in 2025 by Reach Sport.

www.reachsport.com
@Reach_Sport

Reach Sport is a part of Reach PLC.

Hardback ISBN: 9781916811201
eBook ISBN: 9781916811218

Photographic acknowledgements:
Alamy, Rowan Griffiths

Cover Design: Chris Collins
Editing and production: Simon Monk, Christine Costello

Every effort has been made to trace copyright.
Any oversight will be rectified in future editions.

Printed and bound by CPI Group (UK) Ltd,
Croydon, CR0 4YY.

MIX
Paper | Supporting
responsible forestry
FSC
www.fsc.org
FSC® C013604

My wonderful wife, who inspires me every minute of every day.

FOREWORD

BY GARY PENRICE

I'VE known Ollie for more than 50 years now.

At different times we were teammates – from the age of 10 through to 35 – up to when I retired from playing and became part of his staff. I have worked with Ollie in various roles and at different times over the past 25 years.

Ollie has endured many challenges over that time, on and off the field, all of them met with a resilience and inner strength that defines his character, always pushing himself and trying to find new ways to succeed, even after what might have been judged as failure.

He made 597 appearances as a player and now has overseen more than 1,000 games as a manager after taking on the Swindon Town job – this is testament to his commitment and dedication to the football industry.

Knowing Ollie as I do, it's not the promotions, countless playoffs, (wins and defeats) or relegations that he will have missed while he was out of the game – it's the helping people and changing mindsets that he loves, basically, imparting his enthusiasm, experience and knowledge into the team and club environment.

Football is a roller coaster of emotions and to have shared some of those highs and lows with Ollie has been a privilege.

I'm looking forward to reading what Ollie has to say about anything and everything because he has experienced a hell of a lot in his life and career and experience is a great thing to hand down.

I have an old Mark Twain saying that sums up Ollie perfectly, 'It doesn't matter the size of the dog in the fight, it's the size of the fight in the dog.'

That, to me, is Ollie.

Enjoy the book… I'm certain you will!

Gary Penrice
March 2025

INTRODUCTION

IN 2006, I was asked whether I wanted to put my life down on paper and in truth, I was initially reluctant. I'd been asked to do an autobiography several times before, but after giving it some thought, the timing felt right, and I agreed to do it. I had a few ghostwriter options, but the publisher put forward a lad who lived in Manchester.

I was manager at Plymouth Argyle at the time and so I said I'd like to meet him first to see how we got along. I suppose that was my first test to see how much he really wanted to work with me, because that really mattered.

A few days later, I met him at Plymouth train station. I discovered he had three young children – and he told me he hoped our meeting would go well because he really wanted to help me with my book.

I told him the fact he'd travelled from Manchester to Plymouth to see me was good enough as far as I was concerned, as he had the job if he still wanted it.

Over the course of the next six months or so, we wrote what eventually became *Ollie* together and that book sold pretty well. I enjoyed the process and recall doing a few chapters in warm sunshine in the garden that my wife Kim and I had overlooking Plymouth Hoe.

My ghostwriter kept in touch, and over the next few years I moved on to Leicester City and then Blackpool. We updated the paperback after Blackpool won promotion a few years later in 2021, and he came back to me with another idea that eventually became *How to Be a Football Manager*. The book was shortlisted for the Sports Entertainment Book of the Year category at the Sports Book Awards in 2023, it sold well, and again people seemed to really like it.

In 2024, my ghostwriter – who is a shy lad and likes to stay in the background – asked me again about a third book. His pitch was pretty simple – how would I fancy giving my opinion on anything and everything? I asked him whether he thought people would want to hear what I thought about anything and everything. He, and Reach Sport, the publisher of this book, believed they would. I hope they are right!

So, here we are!

We wanted to create a football book that was like no other in that, to my knowledge. Nobody in football has done a book of this type before – though I'm happy to be corrected. There are a few 'World According To…' type of tomes out there and I'm flattered to join people like Jeremy Clarkson, David 'Bumble' Lloyd and a few others.

So, what exactly have we put together?

Well, it's a collection of random observations, thoughts, opinions and stories, as mentioned above, about anything and everything. Wherever possible, and quite often, if it is not a football story *per se*, I will try and loop it back to the beautiful game.

The topics were presented to me randomly with no preparation or research at my end. I literally had no idea what I would be asked about for each of the many interviews we did – that's the way I wanted it because I wanted a feeling of spontaneity and my reactions to be natural, off the cuff and as genuine as possible.

Also, the aim of this rag-tag collection of thoughts, insights and responses was that you would never quite know what was coming on the next page.

You, the reader, will decide if we've achieved our goal. We want it to be a fun, easy read with a few life lessons I've learned sprinkled in that I hope help people. There are a few topics that are not light-hearted, but I'm glad I got to share my opinion about them.

And you might not agree with everything, but that's absolutely fine. You'll know the ones when you come to them.

There are a couple of nuggets that we've decided to include from my previous books, just because they make me smile and they are often mentioned to me by the people who have been kind enough to buy my other books. Otherwise, it's my thoughts and views on this mad, infuriating but wonderful world we live in – and more often than not, connected in some way to the profession I am proud to earn my living in.

From eccentric kit men to ghosts. From tea ladies to cats and dogs. From UFOs to moments in football that I will never forget – or in some cases live down.

So, onwards and forwards. I hope you enjoy reading the pages that follow as much as I enjoyed providing the wit and wisdom (my wife Kim might disagree with that description) that fills them.

We toyed with organising the topics into chapters, or alphabetising the categories – but in the end, just decided to include them in the order they were asked.

Hope you enjoy it!

Ian Holloway,
The Cotswolds, February 2025

PLAYING FROM THE BACK

IN football, there's no right or wrong way to do anything. Every team can play the way they want to, have their own identity and try and win matches the way they believe is best for their club.

The Wimbledon team of the 1980s had their own way – by being direct and physical. Nobody liked playing them, which is ironic because I joined them as a player for one season and hated it from start to finish.

Stoke City, under my old mate Tony Pulis, had their own way of playing and it was effective and feckin' difficult to play against. Ask Arsene Wenger!

What I can't understand today, is why every team wants to play the same way, and that is the 'Pep Guardiola Way' of playing it out from the back and working your way upfield.

Pep has – through no fault of his own – made it unfashionable to play any other way, but if my team played against Manchester City, and I tried to play the same way without the in-depth knowledge that he has of playing in that fashion, I'd be letting myself and my players down badly.

I'd have to draw from my own knowledge and if you do something different from somebody else, that doesn't make you wrong and it could give you enough of an advantage to actually win.

As a coach, you need to look at the skillsets your players have and ask if you are playing to their strengths? Because if you're not and they are making mistake after mistake after mistake, you're not a very good coach, are you? You'll also find yourself out of work pretty quickly.

I must have turned my TV off about 10 times last season because I got so sick and fed up with watching teams trying to play in somebody else's style and getting it totally and utterly wrong, making mistake after mistake but persisting with it anyway.

I believe coaches who try and play Pep's way are missing the real genius behind his tactics. The magic of Pep's team is that they try to win the ball back as quickly as possible as a unit and not be susceptible to counter-attacks. That's his priority. The best team in the Premier League without the ball, is Manchester City – week in, week out – they try to win the ball back off you the moment they lose it and they do it against everyone. (Although as I write, things seem to have been a bit more difficult in the 2024/25 season!)

People talk about the way Pep's team plays, but they aren't looking at the bigger picture because how City are without the ball is hardly ever mentioned and it infuriates me because that isn't his focus 90% of the time.

What a wonderful talent Leroy Sane was for City – but he never did what Pep wanted him to do when he didn't have the ball, so he got rid of him. When he had it, he was brilliant, but that wasn't good enough for Pep because I believe he judges a player without the ball as much or even more than when he does. I believe that's what his philosophy is, so all of this playing out from the back is flawed because that's not what it is all about. And if you are a struggling League Two side, you are not suddenly going to start playing like Manchester City because you try and play the same way.

It's mind-blowing how Pep has figured all this out.

Having different philosophies in football is good and quite entertaining.

Muhammad Ali used to find different ways to win fights. He'd figure out what his opponents' strengths and weaknesses were and adjust his style accordingly.

At Blackpool, we had a particular way of playing that I felt suited the lads I had and that involved huge switches in play – I was insistent about that and worked on something I believed in, and we had an ethos that equated to this: if we lost the ball, we had to win it back within four seconds if we could.

International football has become incredibly boring because all nations – bar Spain – all want to play the same way, including Gareth Southgate's England, which in fairness, Gareth had a fair amount of success with.

Liverpool used to have a saying years ago that there is no long ball or no short ball, just the right ball at the right time and that's what Pep does – and he's got a goalie in Ederson who is one of the best passers in the world and has more Premier League assists than any other keeper over the past 30 years.

If you've got a keeper who you play it back to and he can't hit an accurate long ball, you're in trouble. Look at Joe Hart – a wonderful goalkeeper capable of fantastic saves – but couldn't do what Pep wanted him to, so he moved him on, even though he was England's No.1 at the time! That takes some guts.

Pep is the only manager in my lifetime who has changed everyone else's thinking and that's not a good thing in my opinion, because he has a bespoke side designed to play the way he wants. Yes, your team should be comfortable on the ball, but you should also have your own ideas.

As an example, as Swindon Town manager we took on Carlisle United in January 2025 who were bottom at the time. Mike Williamson was their manager, and they kept playing from the back and we kept catching them out with the traps and high press we had. He had a big lad at the back who couldn't head it, and we ended up winning 5-1 at Brunton Park.

Afterwards, he complained that we'd scored some of our goals from long kicks over the top, but why wouldn't we try a tactic they couldn't defend? I don't wish anyone out of a job, but Mike lost his shortly after and you can't help wondering if persisting with playing it out from the back with players who technically weren't good enough to do that was his eventual downfall.

I see non-League teams doing the same thing, junior sides and even Sunday League teams – it's become an unhealthy obsession.

My advice? Mix it up, take inspiration from others but play to the strengths of the players at your disposal.

DOGS & CATS

NOBODY should be without one, in my opinion. A dog or a cat, that it is.

I've had dogs all my life and the unconditional love you get from them is ridiculous.

Every morning they greet you as if they are seeing you for the first time. It's just the best feeling in the world because no matter how bad your day has been, you are the best thing in their life and they let you know that each and every time. My dogs have all been completely different characters.

We've got two small dogs now, both with massive personalities. Sometimes they leave things around the house they shouldn't and might put little walnut whips here and there – I had one in a pair of my trousers not so long ago – but you get so much back from them it's untrue.

Our little Chihuahua – he finishes our coffee in the morning, pinches Kim's baguette on occasion and is a bundle of mischief, but they're an absolute joy to have around… until they get old and start pissing and shitting all over the place. But it's all part of the fun, isn't it?

When they're asleep, they're not worried about anything, are they? They don't have a care in the world so long as they get to see the occasional squirrel, chase it around the tree or get to chew on a bone, and that's about it.

I've held all our dogs when they passed. I had a Jack Russell called Milo who was 14 and I felt him leave the world as his soul left his body. I can't explain what that felt like, but it was quite wonderful.

It's amazing how each one leaves a mark on your heart, isn't it?

Cats are great, too, but they're more elusive, occasionally devious and vindictive. Do you know they love you as much as a dog does? It's hard to tell because they're that much more independent. Whatever happens with a cat, it's usually on their terms.

Would I rather be a dog or a cat? There's a question!

I think I'd rather be a dog because they give more affection, and they get more affection – cats are too knowing, and they look like they've been here for feckin' years.

I had two cats growing up – Sooty and Dibble. Sooty was all black and Dibble was ginger and thick as a canteen cup who turned into a savage beast towards the end.

You're either a cat person or a dog person, I believe, but if you want a cuddle from a cat, you don't always get one if they're not in the mood. There's the odd one who could send you to A&E if they're not in the mood.

I've had loads of other animals over the years, including budgies, parakeets, goldfish, guppies, chickens and turkeys. There isn't a lot going on with turkeys, if I'm honest – the male one just sort of stood looking at himself in the mirror all day.

Until Christmas, that is!

SWEEPER-KEEPERS

I FIRST came across this phenomenon just after my dad passed away.

I was only 35 and player/manager of Bristol Rovers at the time and my dad was a local football fanatic who everybody knew and respected. So when my old club Longwell Green Juniors approached me to name their annual five-a-side trophy the 'Bill Holloway Trophy' in honour of my dad, I agreed without hesitation and better still, entered a Rovers side I believed would win it.

I entered my strongest team because it was in my dad's name, but we couldn't actually win it because of Bath City. They had entered a side that had a sweeper-keeper who used to play outfield before he decided to become a goalie. It was quite a good pitch the tournament was played on, but because this guy didn't stay in goal, it was like they had six players rather than five and he was so bloody good, they ended up winning it three years in a row. It drove me insane!

I'm going to have to return to Pep Guardiola, here. What Pep's done is tweaked the standard goalkeeper role and twisted it so it seems there is an extra player at the back, and I don't know how they get time to dive or make saves. I've watched some of the very best sweeper-keepers in warm-ups – Ederson, Alisson, David Raya, Manuel Neuer – and they are pinging 60-70 yards balls… to feet!

When I was younger, in knockabouts you'd stick a big bloke – often overweight – in goal as a form of punishment and we'd be horrible to them – 'Just shut your pie hole and get in goal.' But it's fair to say those days are gone.

It's like having midfielders in goal that can do both – play outfield and stop the ball going onto the net – but it only started to come into the game when the back-pass rule changed, and keepers could no longer pick up a pass from their own players.

I actually played in the first ever game where the back-pass rule was changed when I was at QPR. We were away to Manchester City in what was also Sky Sports' first Monday Night Football match, and I remember a City player played it back to Tony Coton who picked it up. For a moment, the City players looked sheepish, the crowd fell silent and the referee totally ignored it!

The back-pass rule was brought in to stop time wasting – I'm not sure it does in reality – and that fundamental ruling has changed the art of goalkeeping forever.

Do you think keepers would need to be that good with the ball at their feet if they could still pick it up? You couldn't even press them high as they could just pick it up and volley it back over your press.

When a sweeper-keeper is at the top of their game, what they can do is a thing of beauty, but there are only a handful who can do it well and effectively.

FISHING

FISHING? I've had one go and that's it.

I went out with Jimmy Bullard on a freezing cold morning, and we didn't even get one bite between us.

I get it, with the game of trying to outthink them, and never knowing if you'll catch anything… and people who love fishing are passionate about it. And I get the challenge and I've seen stuff on TV with cameras on riverbeds and it's incredible how clever these fish are.

I always used to think the hook must hurt them, but I've been assured it doesn't – but I'm not sure I'd enjoy a hook through my lip. Could you imagine if you were offered a nice kebab on a Saturday evening and as you bit into it, somebody suddenly reeled you into the air because you'd taken the bait they'd set and dragged you away? I wouldn't be happy, I have to say!

I love *Gone Fishing* with Bob Mortimer and Paul White-house, but I just think I'd lose my rag really quickly if I went on a regular basis because I don't have the patience you need to do it.

Maybe I should give it another go and if I caught one, perhaps that's what gets you hooked so to speak, but that thrill isn't really one for me at the moment.

ONLINE TROLLS

ONLINE trolls… where to begin? They're all cowards and sadly, it's part of today's world.

I was taught to talk to people, not about them anonymously.

I love the fact that anybody can become famous these days by working hard on their own social media channels or on YouTube – I really do believe it's great.

We've got free speech and there are a lot of very bright, talented people out there who are finding ways to an audience that they might not have had 20 years ago.

But why do we have to have people who can hide behind a keyboard and say what they like about these people and get away with it without punishment? What satisfaction are they getting out of that? I don't get it.

Trolls lurk in the shadows like the nonentities they are – who are these cowards? It's absolute nonsense and I would say you shouldn't listen or read the comments if it happens to you, but they do it so they're in your face and it's very difficult to ignore.

But you have to ignore them, let it go and try and move on.

Are we ever going to eradicate trolls from our lives? I don't think so – but I'd like to speak to the ones who do it and tell them to their face that they are the lowest of the low. The dregs of society and if you were on fire, I wouldn't throw a bucket of water over you. That sounds harsh, doesn't it, but we are talking about people who sometimes drive their victims to take their own lives. You should have empathy for someone else if you are a real human being.

For anyone who is being trolled, don't look at it, don't read it and ignore it – don't give it the time of day.

True criticism is fine, because it makes you stronger and you can learn from it, but trolling is for people who are nasty individuals, cowards and really, do I want them in my book? Not really, so I'll end this by saying this to any trolls out there – you're vile and a genuine waste of a human being.

Jog on.

PUSHY PARENTS

MY dad wasn't pushy, but he influenced me in a massive way. Some people might have called that pushy, but I don't believe I would have been where I am today without him behind me. Mum accepted the way Dad was, but she provided a balance.

If you've got two pushy parents, I feel for you.

Some of the best people in the world had pushy parents, whereas some might have been ruined by them.

Michael Jackson had pushy parents which you could argue ruined his childhood and the Williams sisters in tennis certainly did, but they seem happy enough with their multi-millions in the bank!

One thing I can't understand is the American pageants where they dress six-year-olds up as though they are 25 – OMG – have a look at yourself! What's all that about? That's not right in my book.

It's all about how you deal with it. Deep down, they are only wanting the best for you, so anyone who has a pushy parent, when you are older, you'll totally understand what they were trying to do.

But you have to step up and say what you think is best for you and you shouldn't be led by them – and that's a big moment in your life.

Lewis Hamilton's dad had three or four jobs in order to fund his go-karting and early race career, but as he made his way in F1, he had to effectively sack him as his manager in order to progress with his career.

It's great if you end up being successful in whatever you do – look at the Murrays – would you call Andy's mum Judy pushy or supportive? I'd definitely go with supportive, but if your parents are over-critical of what you are doing and it's putting you off, that's the time to tell them 'It's my life, not yours.'

I always think that an awful lot of parents just try to give you that little quarter-turn on the screw of life, so you have a bit more than they had, but it's easy to overdo it if you have a power drill in your hands!

It's a very fine balance. You want to be nurtured, not neutered! You want to be assisted, you want to be prompted, and you want to be cherished and encouraged, but you don't want to be forced.

I've seen both sides of it as a manager. I had a player who I was trying to tell to do something one way, but his dad was telling him to do it differently and was following him around wherever he went. I had to sit them both down and say, 'He's only going to get in my team if he does what I want, not what you want'. Unfortunately, he didn't agree with me and things didn't go well after that.

Listen to your mum and dad, express yourself but do it your way.

And I would imagine it's really difficult following in the footsteps of a famous parent with pressures and expectations placed on your shoulders, but you just have to be yourself and be your own person.

Ultimately, live your life the way you want to.

SUPER JACK GREALISH

WHAT a bloke. Jack has empathy by the bucketload and understands other human beings and he seems to care about everybody.

He has seen how his younger sister has had to fight and battle past so many hurdles just to enjoy her life.

He's seen it, he cares, he understands and he has a balance in his life. I think he's absolutely outstanding as a human being.

So, why does he get booed wherever he goes? I can only think it's jealousy. It's so easy to say 'oh, he's this and that' or 'he's done this or that' – what about all the good things he's done?

I don't start with the bad things about anyone, only the good and I think Jack does so much for other people who aren't as fortunate as he is.

I've always been a Jack fan, he's such an individual with his socks down and hairstyle. I admit, I have hair envy of Jack – he has a magnificent set of curtains! But he also has a smile and it's a real one.

Ian Wright has similar qualities and I've seen that with my own eyes, helping kids and doing whatever he can for those who need it most and Jack has those same qualities – he has a heart of gold.

He just gets it and it's not pity, it's genuine love. He pays back what he has in his life over and over each and every day.

I don't pity my three daughters who are all deaf, I'm just proud of them and sometimes you have to live with someone who has disabilities to realise just how goddamned lucky you are.

But I won't have a bad word said against Jack Grealish.

CLUB CATS

OCCASIONALLY, you'll go to a club that has an unofficial mascot – one that most people will never get to see because it's more of a behind-the-scenes, staff thing.

The 'club cat' is not an unusual thing and I know Man City once had one with its own Twitter account called Wimblydon! Apparently, he was some stray that used to visit the club's Carrington training complex which is in a semi-rural spot just off the M60 in Manchester. I got told he once brought a mouse to Kevin Keegan's office when he was in charge! Maybe his best signing!

The only one I came across at one of my clubs was a black cat called Jude at QPR. It was a long time ago, and he was stray that used to wander into Loftus Road and after every home game, 'Jude' would appear and the staff would try and get him to leave, but eventually they started giving him some bits of food and he ended up moving into the offices as a permanent resident. They knew it was called Jude because it said so on his collar, but despite numerous attempts to reunite Jude with its owner, nobody ever came forward to claim him, hence him becoming a ground cat. Thinking about it, he had one of the most expensive houses in Shepherd's Bush!

Jude became so popular that I think when he eventually

climbed that big scratching pole into the sky, they replaced him with another black cat and that tradition has continued ever since. Jude became the club's official mascot a few years back and it all stemmed from that little stray all those years ago.

I've had plenty of clubs where there's been rats in the boardroom – and most clubs have them! They probably need club cats more than anyone else! Ha!

KARMA POLICE

DO I believe in karma? Yes I do, and it can be a real bitch if you're on the wrong end of it!

There's a witch's saying, apparently – 'beware the lore of three, because whatever thee give out comes back to thee times three'.

I'm married to a white witch, and she firmly believes the energy you give out comes back to you.

So, be careful what you do and see because according to Mrs Holloway, it's likely to come back and bite you on the arse.

Case in point, my old mate Gary Penrice. Things were going well for me at QPR at the time and one game that sticks in my mind was all down to the wit and wisdom of the one and only 'Pen'. We were playing Swindon Town in an FA Cup third round tie at Loftus Road, and we beat them 3-0. I had a bit of a good game that night and Pen scored, too, so we were both quite happy on the journey home afterwards. I was driving and Pen says, 'Ol, I'm starving, pull over.'

So I pulled up outside a fast food restaurant outlet and he asked me if I wanted anything – I wasn't hungry so said 'no'.

'Go on, have some.'

'No, I don't want anything, you nugget.'

Pen has an annoying habit of not listening to you, so I

shouldn't have been surprised when he came out with two boxes, one for him, one for me. 'There you go, mate.'

'I told you I didn't want anything for feck's sake.'

'Go on, have it.' And more fool me, because I did. I know I didn't have to, but he'd talked me into it. A day later and I was shitting through the eye of a needle. I had the military two-step – I couldn't be more than two steps away from the toilet! I was being sick, too, and I couldn't go into work. It was that bad that I went to see my GP and he told me I'd got food poisoning. Cheers, Pen!

I called him up and told him and a bit later, he came round to see me. He couldn't stop laughing at me. I'd been laid up for two days and had lost a stone. It was before a trip to Middlesbrough and Pen says, 'Jesus, Ol – you've lost some weight haven't you? You look like a nose with eyes.'

To be fair, he was right! He carried on taking the piss and I said, 'I didn't even want it, you feckin' idiot.'

He carries on laughing and says, 'How's your luck, then. You get the dodgy one, I get the good one.'

As it turned out, he played at Middlesbrough and this time, his luck was out because he broke his leg in that game, and a few days later, his wife drove him round to see me. He had a full leg cast on and was on crutches, and as soon as he saw me he said, 'Oh, you don't have to say it! I took the piss out of you and here I am. You don't have to say it.'

I said, 'Well, that's great isn't it? I'd rather have what I've got than what you've got. In a week I'll be fine, you idiot.'

Pen sees the funny side of everything and he's a nightmare, but a great mate, and totally irrepressible. One in a million, in fact. But the Karma Police? They're always watching.

GHOSTS!

I COMPLETELY believe ghosts exist, whatever they are.

When I took over at Swindon Town, I discovered our training ground was allegedly haunted. Apparently, it's built on some sort of ancient burial ground and during my first meeting there, this heavy old wooden door opened by itself.

To open it, you have to push down on this big handle, but this swung open on its own and one of the lads said, 'Oh that's the ghost come to say hello, gaffer.'

They have a picture of a poltergeist smashing through a wall and tell me it throws glasses off the bar and the people who work there are scared of it – but I love it.

One of the best ghost stories I was told was from one of the most influential people in my life for many years – Gerry Francis.

Gerry had been my boss at Bristol Rovers, then bought me with his own money at QPR and had been a mentor for more than 40 years.

I was speaking to Gerry one time, and we were discussing Kim's psychic ability and sensitiveness to the strange and unusual.

I told him she sat up in bed at 4am one time and said, 'Oh, my gran's just died.' Four minutes later, we got a phone call to say exactly that, but Kim had just seen her in her dream, waving goodbye to her.

Gerry went all quiet, and white as a sheet. I asked what was wrong and he said, 'Well, I've seen a ghost, but I don't really want to talk about it.'

Eventually, after a bit of cajoling, he took a deep breath and said, 'OK, I was playing for Crystal Palace at the time and was sharing a room with Vince Hilaire.

'There was a prankster in the squad who would get up to this and that, and one of the things he did was knock on your room door and then run off. On this occasion, there was a knock on the door, and I expected it to be him. But when I opened it, there was a white cloaked figure that screamed and ran towards me.'

'I thought it was this teammate of ours messing about so I kung-fu kicked at it, but kicked absolutely nothing and it went straight through me and straight through the bedroom wall. I asked Vince, who had a pillow in front of his face, if he'd just seen what I had.

'He nodded and described exactly the same thing I'd seen and said he was terrified. I did a bit of research afterwards and found that nobody would normally stay in that room because of things that had been seen or heard in it in the past. Normally, they didn't let it out to guests at all because of previous complaints, but because they'd overbooked, me and Vince ended up in there. So, it's not a case of if I believe in ghosts Ollie, I know they are real.'

Quite a story! Gerry is still scared of what he saw that time all these years later and wasn't comfortable telling us about it either.

More recently, Kim and I rented an Airbnb in Wales because I had an after-dinner gig to go to nearby. When I got back, Kim told me she'd felt really nervous alone in the house.

She said, 'You'd better look at this' and she handed me her laptop. She'd looked up the address on Google and found out that a lady had been murdered there. It was somebody who used to sell sweets to the local kids at cost price in what was her own little tuck shop in her front room.

One day, this kid had drunk a load of ale and visited her to get some sweets but decided to rob her instead. She fought him off, but he ended up killing her in her own home – just awful. But Kim had sensed it without any prior knowledge, as if what had occurred there had left some kind of psychic stain, if that makes any sense.

Another time, I was having a dream when I clearly heard my dad shout, 'Get that checked!' It was enough to wake me up and it felt like I'd actually heard him speaking, even though I'd lost him maybe 25 years before.

The thing was, I had a mark on my face at the time and it had been something I'd been worried about for a while. Hearing my dad made me go and finally get the mark checked out and it turned out to be cancer. They treated it, cut it out and I got the all-clear a couple of years later. How can we explain stuff like that?

I always look for signs from those who were close to me but have since passed on. I remember asking my dad just recently for some guidance as I was feeling a bit in limbo with my life. I said out loud, 'What should I do, Dad? I'm missing football – what do you think? Can you help me? Can you guide me? We're rebuilding our house – is that the right thing?'

Then, a few days later, I got an interview for the Swindon Town job, got the position and it's so close to where we live, I didn't have to relocate or anything. To me, it was like 'take this job, stay where you are and build your home'.

Anything is possible, isn't it? We're all still learning about life and possibly even receiving messages, and if that really is a possibility, it's the beautiful thing, isn't it? The question is, do we really want to know everything because chances are, it would blow our minds if we did…

ACCENTS IN FOOTBALL

OH, here we go! Ian Holloway's verdict on accents! So, the question is, can accents hold people back in life? In football, I believe they can and they do.

My accent is a disgrace. I mean that in terms of how I've been perceived over the years like some cider-drinking country bumpkin, and I'm not alone.

There was a lad commentating on a recent England rugby union game who also had a Bristolian accent, and he took the mickey a bit by saying, 'Yeah, after this I'm heading back to Bristol to my council estate with a bit of straw in my mouth.'

Steve Parish, co-owner at Crystal Palace, during a documentary said something along the lines of, 'I spoke to Ian Holloway, and it was all "ooh-arr" this and "ooh-arr" that' – but when he mentioned Dougie Freedman, he didn't do a Scottish accent or take the piss out of him, so why's it alright to do that to me? Am I a farmer? If I was black, would he lay on a thick Jamaican accent? Of course he wouldn't. I can take a joke with the best of them, but if people ever put on a West Country accent, it's usually in some derogatory way and if speaking with a Bristolian twang has held me back, is that fair?

The whole point is you should be allowed to be very proud of where you are from and not have to disguise your accent. Some of us aren't from the best areas, but it really doesn't – or shouldn't – matter.

And what on earth is wrong with the West Country anyway? It's a beautiful part of the world, we have lovely apples and cider and make cheddar cheese for god's sake! Where would you be if you had a cracker and chutney but no cheddar? Come on!

I don't think people from Birmingham who have thick accents get many top jobs, either and it's just wrong because people with accents are no different from anybody else and if people don't like my Bristolian drawl, I couldn't give a monkey's.

The bottom line is we're all trying to be the best version of ourselves and that's what really matters. I wouldn't want to be anyone else, and I wouldn't change a thing about my life. There were times I could have done one or two things better, but that's how it goes.

So, has my accent held me back? You'd have to ask the chairmen, owners and directors of the clubs I didn't get the jobs I was applying for to answer that.

That said, given his new-found Dutch accent when he was interviewed at FC Twente, I am looking forward to hearing Steve McClaren being interviewed as Jamaica's national team manager…

STUTTER PENALTIES

I BELIEVE you should be able to run as far back as you like or from as short a distance as you like in order to take a penalty, but whatever that run up is, it shouldn't be interrupted, in my opinion.

That's not what a penalty is about, is it? It should be the player v the goalkeeper and can you beat the keeper with your shot?

Look at Ivan Toney – he just watches what the keeper is doing and never looks at the ball and he doesn't have a bad record, does he? That's not cheating, it's just being clever and confident. It's unreal and I don't know anyone else that can do that.

I don't think stutter penalties are fair; I don't like them, and boy do I love it when they miss!

GARY LINEKER

HERE'S a cat among the pigeons. Gary's not a nice man in my experience and maybe it was because of my time at Leicester – but all I know is he was horrible to me and, in my opinion, dismissive and disrespectful.

It was while I was at Blackpool I was invited on *Match of the Day*, but it was obvious – in my opinion – Lineker didn't want me there. He didn't speak to me once and didn't even bother saying hello. At the end, I went over and shook his hand and said, 'Hello – maybe you don't want to speak to me because of my time at Leicester, but hello Gary, how are you?'

He said, 'Oh, oh, Ian I wasn't like that.'

I said, 'Yes you were, mate. I know you were.'

A few years later I saw Alan Shearer at Wembley, and he said, 'I loved that time when you forced Gary to shake your hand.' So he could see it, too.

Not my favourite person in the world based on that experience, I have to say.

RADIO PHONE-INS

I DON'T normally listen to after-match phone-ins, but I caught some of *606* with Robbie Savage and Chris Sutton recently and I actually loved it and have now tuned into it quite a few times. It was the football banter between the two of them that made it for me and being an ex-footballer, I completely understand it and miss it if I'm totally honest.

They bounce off each other wonderfully and sometimes, whoever rings in, Robbie and Chris will still be bickering throughout the call. And on one occasion, they carried on their argument – about whether Greece were a good side because they won the Euros, I think – through the entire show and it was brilliant.

People call in because they want a rant about something, but they don't really let them and it's very clever how it all comes together. I don't think I could be as calm as they are. Chris has a habit of winding people up and is the sensible one, whereas Robbie openly says he's crazy, but now he is a manager at Macclesfield, he has a different perspective, and I find it all fascinating.

I've heard Jason Cundy and Andy Goldstein on talkSPORT

and because their show is on late, they can get away with a bit more than pre-watershed programmes.

An ex-Bristol Rovers teammate of mine, Geoff Twentyman, used to have a radio show in Bristol for about 30 years and he'd do Rovers one night, City the next. It was so hard for him because you're dealing with opinions of people and you just have to accept it, whether you agree or not. As an ex-pro, you're going to think your opinion is better qualified and that you're right, but just because somebody has not been a professional doesn't mean they're not entitled to put their thoughts out there and believe that they are correct.

It's just hard when you have been in the game, you know certain things and how they work and have a better understanding of everything – but keeping a lid on that and saying 'actually, I know better' isn't going to really work for a radio phone-in host, is it?

I've never listened to local – or national – phone-ins as a manager after the game. What's the point? Things might be OK while the results are going your way, but once you lose or lose a couple in succession, you'll get someone coming on saying, 'Oh, he's shit, I'd rather have someone else' and then somebody else might call in and agree. You'd become frustrated pretty quickly and it would drive you mad. I'd probably end up calling in myself.

I've done fans' forums at Bristol Rovers, QPR and Blackpool where they've recorded it and later broadcast it, because I always feel it's vital that you're as honest and open as possible with the people who are paying to come and watch you each week.

They don't have access to the sort of information you do, so sharing as much financial info that is allowable, plus what's going on and what you're trying to do is, I believe, crucial.

If they don't have that knowledge – or at least some of it – the only place you are accountable is on the pitch when your team plays and if that doesn't go well, then you're not going to last very long, are you?

I've always felt myself very lucky because I have an opinion on football and I've been paid to use it and run a team with those ideas, which is a privilege.

SIMON JORDAN

I DIDN'T like Simon Jordan before I actually met him. I used to think he was up himself, talked a lot and liked the sound of his own voice, but after speaking to him in person, I changed the way I felt. I think he tells something the way it is, in a very educated way. And what I also like is that he admits he's done wrong in the past.

He's a very clever man and he's the first to say, now that when he was younger and foolhardier, he thought he could do anything, so I like him. He talks a lot of sense, and I like the way he articulates things. I wish I understood every word he says – but I don't and sometimes I have to go and look them up and learn new words – he sounds like he's swallowed a thesaurus because he's got a fantastic vocabulary, and I love how forthright he is.

I think knowing Simon Jordan would be a good thing and I wish I knew him better because I've heard him talk about Neil Warnock and the relationship they had and I'm a tad envious about that, because I wish I had a chairman that would say the same things about me. But at this moment in time, we've never had the chance to work together.

AI
(ARTIFICIAL
INTELLIGENCE)

BE afraid. Very afraid! I don't mind admitting I'm absolutely terrified of AI.

How can we create something that is cleverer than us? And I'll tell you something – if I was the thing that had been created and I found out I was more intelligent than the thing that created me, I'd get rid of it and take over.

I watched *Terminator* years ago and that was terrifying enough. Kim asked why it bothered me so much and I just said, 'That can and will happen one day.' I think we are one or two steps away from that and when you've got Elon Musk creating chips to go into people's brains so they can control computers using their thoughts, then I'm not sure where it's going to end. I don't like the machines he's making, and I saw one recently that made more sense than I did!

I saw two robots playing football the other day and I don't know if it was real or CGI, but they played better than I've ever played in my life! How worrying is that? And that's the future and the way it is going. They even have a robot that is already smarter than Einstein! How can we compete with that?

I'm deadly serious. Since I first saw *Terminator*, I could see where it is all headed and I think there should be some sort of limit on it because when AI starts to have the capacity to control weaponry, I think we're in terrible trouble.

As things stand, it all ends with them getting rid of us, trust me – the machines will take over... and I don't want one of those Arnold Schwarzenegger cybernetic assassins from Skynet chasing me down the high street anytime soon.

ANGE-BALL

I LOVE it. I just wish they were calling it 'Ollie-Ball' because it would be nice given that I tried to do that same style 15 years ago at Blackpool with the high energy press and counterattack. Tony Pulis called it 'Russian roulette football' where he felt my team was taking too many risks, but it was bloody good to watch.

I really like Ange Postecoglou, and I don't think he knows any other way. I heard a pundit recently say that Big Ange needs to learn to manage games, but I'm sorry, the way he manages games is the way he coaches his team every day and every week – he just wants them to think about the next goal.

If the team can't win doing things that way, then they're not good enough. Maybe Ange doesn't get the sort of money to buy players as the other top clubs do, but I think he's a genius in what he's doing.

It's impossible to manage a game, because the other team is going to try and stop you being allowed to manage it – even Man City can't do that all the time. Ange wants his team to keep pressing high, win the ball back and think about the next goal and I'm quite happy with that. I love the fact that he's good enough for people to put a label on it and say that's his style of play.

But how can you criticise his style when he's won a lot of trophies in his career already? He's going to continue winning trophies, too and it's refreshing to see a team trying something different than trying to copy what Pep Guardiola has been doing.

It's entertaining. Would I buy a season ticket to watch Tottenham with Ange in charge? Yes I would, because it's unbelievably good to watch and you could argue that he's not yet managed at the level he deserves. He might still get that if he wins something with Spurs.

I also love the way he talks and how he gets aggressive when somebody criticises him. He believes in what he's doing, which is to create a natural instinct to attack.

You can't play the way he does in half-measures, so he can't have a team that attacks on the front foot and then decides to sit back and soak up pressure. That takes months of coaching and is like asking a lion to chase a gazelle the same way a cheetah would. Lions need to work with other lions to track things and catch them.

If all big cats hunted the same way, there would only be one winner whereas in football, there can be lots of winners and lots of big cats.

What I especially like about Ange is he's out there and good luck to him, because when he takes his last breath, he can quote Frank Sinatra and say, 'I did it my way, mate!'

YOU'RE GETTING SACKED IN THE MORNING

'YOU'RE getting sacked in the morning!'

I hate that chant with a passion. I think it's so disrespectful and an absolute joke.

You turn that around on someone who is going to work and trying as hard as they can to do the best job they possibly can and the second they get something wrong, all the people in the office crowd around their desk singing 'you're getting sacked in the morning'!

I've had some bad moments in my manager career in this area.

I was Bristol Rovers boss when we started to struggle. I'd had to sell my three best strikers and reckoned I was 72 goals down with the loss of Jason Roberts, Bobby Zamora and Jamie Cureton, and I was concerned that we'd not won at home, and we'd failed to win any of our 11 games at the Memorial Ground going into the New Year.

Understandably, the fans were getting a bit restless. I took off a player in one game and then I was treated to a chorus of 'You don't know what you're doing!' Cheers, lads! There's an old saying in football that if you stay at one club too long, you end up smelling of fish and there was a definite waft of a trawlerman's gloves about old Ollie by that point. Captain Birdseye couldn't hold a candle to me!

After that, I felt I would be sacked in the morning.

'Sacked in the morning' is a horrible chant because if any manager hears that, all the eyes of the people in the stadium are on him and it is an incredibly lonely moment for anyone. I think it's totally out of order, it should be banned from being allowed to be sung in a ground and anyone caught doing it should be shot.. or at least have their season ticket taken away.

I'd probably take the shooting option but I'm that bad, I'd probably miss from about a yard away.

PLAYER SCHEDULES

THERE is a lot of discussion and complaints about player schedules of late, but for me, it's a load of bullshit.

For clubs with big enough squads, they should do what Arsene Wenger used to do at Arsenal and throw the kids in and give them a chance in certain competitions.

The higher level games you play, the better and fitter you're going to become, and I don't think burnout comes into it. And if you have to play one player in every single game, there's something wrong with the rest of your squad.

I think, 'just shut up and play the game' – especially when you consider how much some of the players at top clubs are earning – it's a total insult to people who have to work five years to equal one of their week's wages.

I know we shouldn't compare it that way, but you cannot then moan about having to play too much because it's nonsense.

Tennis players sometimes have to play five-hour matches and then have to go out and play again a day later – and nothing is more intense than tennis, is it?

I've seen tennis players train and it's absolutely mental, the fitness levels they have to get to – and their recovery time is hardly anything compared to football.

They can play 30-plus shot rallies, hitting the ball at 100mph – and they only have 30 seconds between points and the ball is hardly ever out of play, so how fit are they? You never hear them moaning about having too many tournaments. And it's not a team game like football where half the time you're having a rest!

The better you are, the fitter you are and the better you will become because when you're tired, you start to lose control of the football and your decision-making is worse. So being fit is a huge part of it.

Talk of strikes is being fuelled by the media and journalists trying to get a headline – I've never heard of a player saying they will strike and if they've answered a question about it, their response has been blown out of all proportion. It's bullshit, in fact.

The managers who have complained about playing a Champions League game on a Wednesday and then a Premier League game at 12.30 on a Saturday are right – the league should back our clubs and say actually, choose another game because that one is being moved to Sunday.

There should be a minimum amount of time between games – maybe 72 hours – and the same at Christmas when there seems to be a game every two days over the festive period. That doesn't make sense to me as a manager and didn't when I was a player. I could be wrong here, but is the first thing everyone thinks about at Christmas, 'let's go to a football match'? Games at that time of the year used to be local derbies for the benefit of all concerned, but now you could be travelling anywhere in the country.

Time limits – whether measured in days or hours – could

solve a lot of problems, and we should be doing everything we can to help our clubs in Europe, but too many games and being tired? I'm not having it. In my experience, players want to play all the time. It's a short career so why wouldn't you want to make the most of something that you love doing?

FOOTBALL HEAD COACHES GETTING YOUNGER

I THINK you should always have new blood coming in, but you also shouldn't disrespect knowledge. Some of us – and I'm including myself – have a lot of experience and knowledge of the game and that shouldn't just be discarded, which seems to be quite a modern thing.

I have no idea why older managers are not getting jobs these days – and I can think of a dozen or more with years and years of management experience. I know there are a load of new exams coming out and that relationships with the media, your presentation skills with fancy graphics to show off during job interviews as well as having as many certificates, diplomas and badges as you can carry, but that doesn't automatically give you the qualifications to go out there and manage a football team.

I think it's a fad to bring in somebody inexperienced – as well as being a lot cheaper – because if for instance you're poaching a Bundesliga Under-21 manager, you're not going to have to pay a fortune to manage in the Premier League, Championship or wherever. And I think some of these owners are looking at these young coaches and thinking, 'hang on, I'm going to be able to control you' whereas if they take on somebody who has been around a while, chances are they are not able to do that quite as easily.

You have to question a lot of new owners and the direction they want their club to go in – is it for the fans or is it because they're getting something out of it? They choose the managers, and they surround themselves with people – many of whom have never worked in football before. As for CEOs – they're everywhere! And how many people are between the owner and the manager? They are a legion! The most successful managers don't need to be surrounded by those types, unless they choose to be.

It might take an older manager to come back in and be successful and then that might start a trend in the opposite direction – and hopefully, that might be me!

Us older managers are like fine wines – we get better with age. It's just being given the opportunity to prove that.

THE RETURN OF THE MULLET

YOU see them everywhere now, don't you and I love them. In fact, I used to have one.

If I could get a stick-on mullet, I'd definitely do it because that was my era, and I miss mine terribly. My old mate Gerry Francis has had a mullet for 40 years or more, and he still has it today, proving that if you persist with something long enough, it will come back into fashion. I wouldn't recognise Gerry without one.

I remember the lead singer of the glam rock band The Sweet – Brian Connolly – he had a corker. Fashion goes around and around. The bubble perm will be next, trust me.

I used to have wavy hair, but now it's just waved goodbye. One minute it was there, the next it had gone. I used Wash and Go, and I watched it go – it even says so on the bottle.

My belief is that every hairstyle will suit somebody – it's just matching them up that's the problem.

As for the best hair in football today, it's got to be Mikel Arteta, all day long. I call him 'Lego man' because he has Lego hair. You can't see the join, either! I saw him turn around the other day and his hair was still pointing forwards because it hadn't moved. It looks plastic and best kept out of the sun, and I'd love to touch it just to see if it's real.

Don't worry Mikel, I'm only jealous. Like the saying goes, hair today, gone tomorrow…

THE SAUDI PRO LEAGUE

I'M afraid to say that I always saw this coming.

The Saudis think they can do what they want and think they can buy what they want and so far, they pretty much have. Let's be honest, they've got the 2034 World Cup, and they're used to having their own way because money talks.

When you look at the money some of these lads are on out there, it's life-changing and they won't have anything to worry about when they retire. I can assure you, when you're an older footballer – particularly in my era where the money wasn't there – you end up worrying what you're going to do for the rest of your life.

Unfortunately, an awful lot of players haven't had a good life when their career ended, with no source of income and mental health issues because they used to do something they were really good at, everyone liked it and then all of a sudden, it just stops, and you can lose yourself.

So, I don't blame anybody who gets the chance to secure their future, and takes that opportunity to do that when it arises.

The question is whether anyone wants to watch those leagues

and whether playing in surroundings and a culture that is completely alien to them can be sustained by what's coming out of those oil fields?

It's a very different way of life out there and not one I think I'd particularly like because I like old, traditional things and places.

I like a good flea market or charity shop whereas everything they have is bling, posh, crisp and modern-looking.

People in that part of the world love their sport, and they want everything and everyone to come to them and as I say, normally, they get what they want.

To summarise, I'd say if that's what they want, good luck to them – do it. But I'd be very wary if you're a young enough fella, that it also doesn't damage your career because money isn't why we all started playing, is it?

Money comes to you, if you're good at football. You earn it and can enjoy it at the end of your career when you've earned it – but this is the wrong way around, where players are being given riches beyond their wildest dreams while they are mid-career. Because football is in a terrible position if you are making someone famous and rich before they are really famous and rich – if that makes sense – and you don't have the experience of life to handle untold wealth at such a young age, so there are many pitfalls for young footballers to face by making the choice of playing in Saudi.

One example I'll give is Ruben Neves – I don't understand why he's gone out to Saudi at his age? Jordan Henderson, I could fully understand and Stevie G – he saw Aston Villa rocket after he'd gone and he was probably thinking, 'hang on a minute – where am I going here? Where am I headed?' If you've made yourself a name, use it and do it because he was only gaining wasn't he? But I'd question Ivan Toney's decision because he'd just come off the back of the Euros where he'd played and made an impact for England so this was his chance to shine – career-wise, I don't get why he'd move to the Saudi Pro League because the reality is nobody really cares what happens in that league. Do 40 goals a season in the Saudi Pro League make people sit up and take notice?

Money makes everything tick and unfortunately that's the way it is, and I suppose we're all after getting on that gravy train because you've got to look after the chicks in the nest, so do I blame them? No. Do I want this exodus to happen? Probably not, because I want football to be as pure as it can be but I'm realistic enough to know that the money on offer is a huge draw. How can anyone compete with the richest nation on the planet?

I wish I could find an oil well under my property! And if I did, I'm not sure I'd want to pay footballers around the world to come and play in a league that is still crap! I think of Pele – my all-time favourite player – when he was at Santos. He was so much better than the standard around him and he was like a beacon in amongst it all. So if you're a really good footballer, you want players around you that are your equal or better, so you can rise to that level. If it's the opposite and you're a good player but the majority of those around you are at best average, how can you improve or reach your best levels when you know if you give 60% that will likely be more than enough?

I can't ever see the Saudi Pro League attracting enough young players to be a legitimate quality league. I watched David Beckham's brilliant documentary on Netflix and he spoke about when he went to play in the MLS in the USA. He couldn't handle it because the levels of professionalism weren't what he was used to.

The Premier League is the best league in the world and the

Saudi Pro League will never be able to compete with it – unless they started taking all of our best players over there and then I'd be worried. For me, football is all about being the best footballer you can be and if the levels around you aren't what they should be, you'll develop bad habits, you won't improve. That's why the Premier League is so brilliant because we have top players from all around the world who can't wait to come here.

We're too big, the Premier League is too good, and the levels are too high for us to lose players at the right age to the Saudis. If you're 33, 34 or 35, go and fill your boots, but leave too early and you will never be as good as you could have been.

The more it becomes a business, the worse football and sport becomes.

The bottom line is, I don't blame anyone who goes there, but it annoys me at the same time, and it really gets my goat. If that makes sense.

WE lost Kim's dad recently and I recall going to see him several years back in hospital where he was bed-bound. I remember telling him about how the officials kept getting things wrong and how I felt they had it in for me, saying things like 'that was never a penalty' and this that and the other and he just said, 'Ian, until referees have all the angles and you've watched an incident back over and over again, how can you say they're wrong? We need to give them every single angle, and they'll get it right.'

That's what he said, all those years ago – and he was right.

At that time, if you'd go to parks or playing fields up and down the country every Sunday morning to watch grassroots football at every level, you'd see that nobody has any faith in referees because everyone has watched *Match of the Day* and Gary Lineker, and his pundits would slaughter every referee every Saturday night. They'd say, 'he got that wrong or he didn't see that' or whatever because they had all these camera angles to make a judgement.

We've brought VAR technology in and goal-line technology that confirms if a ball has fully crossed the line or not which is fantastic because I used to see moments when I'd think that if there was any doubt if a big club were involved, the goal would be given, where if it was the two-bit club I was managing, the 'goal' wouldn't be given because it was easier for referees and linesmen to go with the flow. That technology takes all that away – or it should do.

Returning to my wonderful father-in-law and what he said, the fact is that referees are still not seeing all the angles unless they are asked to go to the pitch-side monitor, so how can he make an informed decision on a borderline call? We have all this wonderful technology, but we aren't using it correctly yet. We need to look at rugby union and how they handle it and adopt some of their interpretation and rules. So, if you have someone arguing and moaning, the ball is moved 10 yards further forward. Therefore you can't argue with the referee, or you'll pay the price.

I think of it like me and Kim with our grandkids, 'No means no. I've said no so don't ask again and don't ask Nanny because that's the end of it. I've said no and I mean it.'

There are no consequences for players who moan at the referee.

I think it's also vital we don't take the on-field referee's authority away when they go to VAR – he should be going to the VAR for assistance when he is unsure of something, and they can confirm it – sort of like, 'I think he's been fouled in the box, can you check that for me?'

If we can all hear and understand what he's thinking, we all know exactly what is going on. Surely that has to be better for everyone concerned? It doesn't have to just be if something is clear and obvious, it's about using that technology to allow him to do his job to the best of his ability. That is what VAR should be for in my opinion, and they should be doing it a lot quicker because rugby is used to breaks of play in their game, while football isn't.

In football, VAR is calling all the shots and taking the authority away from the on-field referee.

The bottom line is that refs in rugby union never lose control and VAR is there to assist him when he needs it. We need to persevere with it and try new ways of implementing the benefits it can provide for officials because if we scrap it and go back to how it was, those marginal decisions will keep going against the smaller clubs and the bigger clubs will keep getting those marginal or even incorrect decisions. We've lost the spontaneity that we used to have, and we need to get that back because waiting to celebrate a goal is ruining the fans' enjoyment.

OFFSIDE – THE LINES ARE DRAWN!

HERE'S one of the most used VAR tasks – was there an offside when the goal was scored? The lines are drawn and sometimes, it might be a toe or an ear that is in an offside position – there have been so many goals ruled out for these reasons. For me, there should be clear daylight between the goal-scorer and the last man, so all your body has to be offside, not just one little bit of it. That way, there would be more goals given and defenders would have to really defend. I want to see more goals given, and fewer chalked off, but to do that we're going to have to change the basic offside rules, and I can't see that happening.

SYSTEMATIC FOULING

THIS should be a straight red card.

The old 'take one for the team' by picking up a yellow card to stop a counterattack, for me, is cheating and you should never gain an advantage by cheating. Any deliberate professional foul should end in a dismissal, and I think it would drastically reduce the amount of times it happens because that player can no longer tug the shirt of the player going past him unless he's prepared to make the sacrifice of his team playing with one man fewer. There are players I can think of who do it regularly and probably would only get 10 games a season if that law came into effect.

I'll go back again to Pele and what he had to put up with. I remember against Uruguay that he got fouled so many times that he ended up going off on a stretcher. He was kicked, wrestled to the ground, pushed and fouled from start to finish and that, my friends, is cheating!

When I was at Palace, Wilfried Zaha looked dejected in the dressing room on one occasion because he couldn't understand why he kept getting kicked and I just said, 'It's because you're so good.' He said, 'Why can't they try and just stop me without fouling?' and I told him because that's what the world is like. Players cheat and it shouldn't be encouraged, should it?

As I say, the consequences for cheating aren't big enough or strong enough and that applies to everyday life, not just football, but when was the world ever run by common sense? I'd have a hall of shame each season for the worst perpetrators and I'd put them in stocks on the village green and have everyone throw rotten fruit at them. We need to make our game as cheat-proof as possible because it has become a case of win at all costs rather than win the right way.

SIMULATION

FOR obvious diving, I'd give a straight red card. It's cheating, plain and simple and what's the point of sport if you're allowed to cheat? I'd have a three-card rule, too, so if a player gets three red cards for simulation, they get a 10-game ban or even more.

Think about other sports. I don't know much (or want to know that much) about cricket, but I know a few years back that Australia's Steve Smith and David Warner were using sandpaper to scratch the ball so it would 'swing' more – wow! The authorities banned them as a result and threw the book at them. They were trying to gain an advantage by effectively cheating, so what's the difference if a footballer takes a dive and wins his team a penalty? That's cheating as well, the consequences for the club on the receiving end could be huge and it should be punished. If you saw a high jump competition and one guy had springs on his heels, there would be outrage – even if it would look fantastic!

So, if you throw yourself to the floor in the box and get a penalty, you have conned the referee and worse still, there's no retrospective punishment when somebody has clearly cheated. How can those players look at themselves? When I was coming through as a player, the older players would slaughter you if you took a dive and started rolling around on the floor – they wouldn't accept it and they'd tell the lad, 'you're not going to make it' because there was a pride and camaraderie about being honourable and not cheating.

There has to be consequences. We've all seen players go down clutching their face as though they've just been levelled by Mike Tyson, and then seen the TV replays showing their face hasn't even been touched, but they get away with it. Nobody questions it and until the consequences for doing that are severe, it's just going to keep getting worse.

It's become a lot more prevalent over the years because that kind of simulation used to be common in foreign leagues, whereas there was a pride in the English game that there was a physicality and an edge, but players got on with it. Gradually, it has crept more and more into our game. I remember watching Spanish football and we'd laugh at them rolling around on the floor before bouncing up unscathed – but now it's over here.

I don't accept it from my lads, and I've had a few rows over the years with players who have done it. I remember at Blackpool when we'd just been promoted, and David Moyes was tearing a shred out of one of his Everton players for rolling around feigning injury.

I heard him in the tunnel as I went to grab a coffee and he was shouting, 'How fucking dare you! Don't ever do that at my football club.'

I find players rolling around holding their face embarrassing – cringeworthy, even. Let's try and stamp it out for the good of the game.

KNOCKING THE BALL OUT FOR AN INJURED PLAYER

WHENEVER this topic crops up, I always think of Marcelo Bielsa and the time he instructed his Leeds United players to concede a goal from kick-off because his team had scored while a Villa player was down injured.

Bielsa is a pure football man, he loves the game, and I don't think anybody thinks about football the way he does because he's absolutely besotted by it.

He's inventive, innovative and even inspired Pep Guardiola, who holds the Argentine boss in the highest esteem.

That's what the game should be about – integrity and compassion.

Who could forget Paolo Di Canio catching the ball when the Everton keeper damaged his knee attempting to make a clearance and he lay in agony? Instead of trying to score as the cross came in, Di Canio jumped up and caught it before pointing at the stricken goalie.

People don't forget moments like that, and with good reason. Sportsmanship means so much to the paying public and sportsmen alike, because that really is what it's all about, as well as being able to be humble when you win or lose.

Sir Alex Ferguson had a 60% win rate, but that means for 40% of the time he was either drawing or losing, but it's about how you do it and how determined you are because that's what affects those around you.

If I felt the game should be stopped for any reason, I'd walk onto the pitch and tell them to kick it out because my players should know my feelings on that. In our team meetings, I would highlight any number of random subjects or topics and get them to share their opinions and thoughts. A bit like this book!

I always wanted to get them thinking, so they had empathy in moments where it's needed and to create a spirit and camaraderie that would ensure they were thinking as one in moments like that.

My lot would have known what I wanted them to be like and how I wanted them to think in any given situation – that's not to say I didn't let them think for themselves – but I wanted to create an environment that they'd all thrive in.

Being honest, doing your best when you play, being humble in triumph and accepting defeat in the right spirit are all commendable traits I try to instil – that, plus not bloody cheating!

PROGRAMME NOTES

I THINK your manager notes in the matchday programme are vital because that's where you can get most of your messages out to the fans. You have to pay the utmost attention to detail with them and make sure the person transcribing gets them absolutely bang on. I think most people understand managers don't have the time to sit down and write them, but it's crucial that you, the manager, then reads them to check what is being put out is bang on and absolutely what you want to say.

For me, they're a huge part of being a manager. I'm not sure how many people actually sit down and read the manager notes, but in my opinion, they should because they'll understand their manager that much better if they do. They're really, really important and a vital line of communication because that's almost the only opportunity we get to speak directly to the supporters.

PLAYERS SHOWING EMOTION

WE see players expressing their feelings more than ever these days. Particularly when you see somebody coming off with an injury they know is bad and you can see them in floods of tears or with their shirts pulled up over their heads. It wouldn't have happened in my playing days but is it a bad thing? Are people allowed to cry? Of course they are. If you've just come back from injury and have a recurrence, I think it's perfectly understandable because you know how tough that is mentally, and you have to face it all over again.

There's nothing worse than being injured in football. Not being picked or being left on the bench is an occupational hazard – but while injuries are as well, they leave players wondering if they will be the same athlete again or whether they will ever get back to where they were before, or even if they will get back in the team.

Training is different as you recover, and you're in at different times and you don't really have time to recuperate because you're always being pushed to get back as quickly as possible. So I fully understand the torture. It's a mental struggle that you have to fight on your own and if you see your replacement in the team is doing well, it's also a major source of worry, so when I see a player crying when they are coming off with an injury, I fully get it.

I can only ever remember crying once in football. It was while I was playing for Bristol Rovers in 1989 and we were in what was then the Division Three play-off final against Port Vale which, unlike now, was played over two legs. We drew 1-1 at Twerton Park and lost the return 1-0 at Vale Park, conceding with just seconds remaining. It was a knife to the heart because we'd given everything that season.

But sometimes, from your lowest moment you can take something very special and there was one thing from that game that, despite the pain and disappointment we felt, still makes me chuckle today. Just after they scored, I was walking back towards the centre spot and I looked over to Gary Penrice as their crowd went bananas, spilling over onto the pitch, and he was laughing and pointing at something.

I thought, 'What's he found so funny?' and looked to where he was pointing to see one of those little turquoise microcars designed to be used by disabled drivers absolutely bombing down the touchline, knocking into fans as it went. Whether the driver was celebrating or trying to keep people off the pitch, I'll never know, but it was surreal and even though I was crest-fallen, I had to laugh because I'd never seen anything like it. We just about kicked off again and the referee blew for full-time.

But it was what was said by Gerry Francis afterwards that stayed with me. We were absolutely shattered, but as we slumped down in the dressing room, Gerry gave one of the most poignant speeches I think I've ever heard from any manager. He said, 'Don't you be ashamed to cry.'

My dad had always told me not to cry and would give me

a whack when I did, but now my 'new dad' was telling us all it was OK and I looked around and there wasn't a dry eye in the place because the thought of all that hard work and the 50 games we'd played had all been in vain, was just too much.

Gerry went on, 'For all those days when you think it's hard, think about every game, think about how fit you need to be and think about how hard we're going to work next year and how we're going to keep this pain in our heart like a burning ember, and make sure we don't ever experience it again. You can do it, you're good enough and we lost out on promotion by one goal. Remember that.'

You could have heard a pin drop by the time he'd finished, and then he told us how proud he was of us all and that we should be proud of ourselves. It felt like a ray of sunshine slicing through your body.

By the end of our coach journey home, I think it was cemented in our minds. It sounds daft, but we knew we wouldn't fail next time. Gerry's words made us focus on what we needed to do. It was inspired stuff and the mark of not only a very clever manager, but a great man, too. We won promotion the following year and I think each and every one of us remembered those tears at Vale Park each and every time we played that season.

HOLES IN SOCKS

THIS is a trend that fascinates me. Clearly the socks the player is wearing are too tight, so, for Christ's sake, make the feckin' socks less tight! Why do they have to vandalise their kit? I just don't understand why the kit companies don't make socks that fit instead of ones that are cramping people's calves. Either that or make them with the holes in already so they don't look like some punk rocker's tights.

I hate it, it doesn't look good and if I brought my grandson a Cristiano Ronaldo full kit for whoever he is playing for at that time, I'd be horrified if I then saw him with a pair of scissors and his new socks. Either the calves in football are getting bigger or the socks are getting smaller, and I can't fathom out which it is.

CLUB MASCOTS

THEY'RE mad, aren't they? Ours at Swindon looks more like a turkey than a robin. I used to enjoy the mascot grand national, and I remember the Bristol City three little pigs had a fight with the wolf from Wolverhampton. It's just a bit of fun but I always wonder if they reveal their true identity to anyone in the same way Peter Parker is Spiderman or Clark Kent is Superman?

They can be an important part of your club's identity, and the kids seem to love them, so I do like it and if the little ones think they are real pigs, wolves or turkeys, then so much the better. If the grand national has stopped, I think it's time they brought it back. I did hear Jude, the QPR black cat mascot was relieved of his duties for showing too much interest in the female Rangers fans – either that or they had him neutered!

JEREMY CLARKSON & CO

I'VE always liked Jeremy Clarkson, even if he is Marmite to the British public. I think people like Jeremy are very easy to dislike and a lot of people will look at him and be a bit jealous because he's in the news all the time and because he comes over as a bit of a know-it-all – for want of a better description.

But I really like him. He never shirks anything, says it like it is and he's a very intelligent man. He doesn't tolerate fools and what he's doing for farming in this country is exceptional. He's bought a farm and gone in there with absolutely no knowledge of what to do, making an arse of himself and getting it all wrong and brought in a farm manager – Kaleb Cooper – who he's made into a celebrity, and I think he's doing brilliantly.

He understands farmers and speaks out for them, using his fame to get the messages across and I think he genuinely appreciates how difficult it is to farm and how committed you have to be. I think he's made an even bigger success of himself than he was before. Just because he's been lucky enough to drive all those wonderful cars and owned a load as well, as I say, there's a certain amount of jealousy towards him, but he also has a lot of people who admire him and respect his appraisals of cars. I could watch him all day long.

It isn't easy to go against the grain and say things that maybe are difficult to hear, and there are others, too. Piers Morgan and Simon Jordan (who I mentioned earlier in the book) are two more good examples. I like what they stand for and though I might not always agree with them, they start healthy debate.

I try to do it myself, maybe in a different way, and I call all of 'us' Marmite because you either like the way we speak out or you don't, with no middle ground. Putting yourself out there and saying things that cause a stir is not an easy place to be at. This book will no doubt have some stuff in you like and agree with and plenty you don't agree with! Like I said, Marmite! Some people love you; some people hate you, but I think it's important that you have an opinion, and you voice it – I just wish I was as eloquent as they were! It's so important to be able to have your say in life because my daughters, who were all born profoundly deaf, haven't been able to.

Human beings are very special because we can communicate in the way we can, whereas deafness takes people away from people. So anybody who has an opinion and is able to voice it as brilliantly as those people we have talked about in this entry, I'm having them all day long. I just find people like that interesting.

THE HAIRDRYER TREATMENT

THIS term is usually 'applied' when someone has 'lost it'. A manager goes absolutely apeshit and loses his composure just because he's trying to provoke a response. I don't really like it, and I haven't really ever done it.

Gerry Francis had a moment with me at Bristol Rovers one time and I probably deserved it. I came in at half-time and we were 2-1 down at Exeter City and he went absolutely ballistic at me. I opened my mouth first saying, 'Come on lads, fucking hell…' and he just said, 'Shut up and get off.' And that was it – I didn't go out for the second half. As the lads were going back out, he said, 'Look, just because you open your mouth doesn't exempt you. You weren't the worst, but I wanted to speak first.' We still lost 2-1 that day.

The Hairdryer Treatment is because you have lost control in many ways and while I don't know anyone who does that deliberately, if you look at Sir Alex, if you didn't do what he was asking you to do, he'd hammer you – but I think that's what he was like anyway. I actually don't think you can do that anymore because it's not acceptable to speak to people in that way. Oh my god – players today are that much more sensitive, it's unbelievable! The culture I was brought up in, it was accepted and just part of the game.

The first time I was on the end of it was when I was just making my way at Bristol Rovers. The Rovers left-back, Lindsay Parsons, picked me up by my collar and slammed me against the wall and said, 'I'm not sure about you, you lazy little get. We don't do that here – we work our socks off.' I said, 'I want to do that. I want to work hard' and he just added, 'Well make sure you bloody well do, son.'

All the senior players were like that. I remember going into the first team dressing room one time because I had to do something and didn't knock and one of the lads said, 'Hey! Who the hell are you? What do you think you're doing? You knock first and then you wait outside! Who the hell do you think you are?' And that's how it was in my playing days. We had more hairdryers than Vidal Sassoon!

In this day and age, it's considered a form of bullying, but back then, bullying was an accepted part of discipline. You just can't do that anymore. Yeah, I raise my voice every now and then, but I always end on a positive – 'Can you do that? We all need you to do that? Come on! You're better than that!' You do that to try and shock them, but if you're lucky, you'll have players out there who will do that during a game, so you can change what's happening and they'll do it in a way that the player knows that his teammates still care about him.

For instance, I've been told that if Roy Keane ever gave you a bollocking, if you responded, he'd always say 'Well done' after-wards. He'd just try to get something out of his team. Even when my Swindon lads went in 4-0 down against Colchester United at half-time a few weeks into my time at the club, I didn't rip into them. I just told them, 'That's not good enough.

You looked like you were scared, and you didn't put the effort in – or were frightened to.' So I changed them around because I don't think shouting and bawling works.

When I was a kid, if I did anything wrong, my dad would hammer me. I wouldn't be allowed out to practice, which killed me, but he knew my currency and in management, it's no different. It's all about knowing the currency and Sir Alex knew he could get under his players' skin, and he had that passion for Manchester United. He was allowed to do things his way without question, because he wouldn't accept second best and would let them know – in no uncertain terms – their place in the grand scheme of things compared to the history of that club.

I imagine he said, 'Who do you think you are? What sort of honour is it to play for this club? How dare you play like that.' He made players understand they were nothing compared to Manchester United and everything that club stands for. So, that's how Sir Alex used his 'hairdryers', and I totally and utterly agree with it.

My way is to take out the anger and generate a feeling of passion and involve my lads in the emotion I'm trying to stir up. If I can show it and feel it and explain how I would have felt and reacted as a player, then they might too. I'd say something along the lines of, 'You wear that shirt with passion. Don't you dare wear that shirt and be afraid to do your job.' And when the lads start to buy into that and use that emotion and passion when they play, things can turn around very quickly.

It's all about staying in control and channelling your anger and emotion into meaningful and relatable instructions. In today's world, if you rant and rave, people switch off, they don't listen, and your message is lost.

A lot of today's players are given a lot of money at a very

early age, and they haven't had to work for it. When I was a player, we used to think, 'If I don't get this right, I'll be out of a job' whereas a lot of top players today have enough money to not have to worry about things like that. So, do they really care? It's a weird scenario for me, and football is the wrong way around. You should have a brilliant career and get the money at the end, not all up front.

RAINBOW LACES & LGBT SUPPORT IN FOOTBALL

AT the end of the day, we're supposed to be an all-inclusive world, but are we really? I don't think we are. I believe the vast majority of people are good natured and fair and we care about everybody else no matter what colour they are or what their sexuality is – unfortunately, the remainder of the world is not that way.

Football should not be a platform where you demonstrate who you care about – and who you don't – because you're representing your football club in everything you do, whether on or off the pitch. To me, that means not conveying any sort of messaging when you're representing your club so if you have your club's armband on, you shouldn't really put your feelings on there to make whatever sort of statement you are trying to make, should you?

How you feel is how you feel but demonstrating it when you should be at work is wrong and you shouldn't use the publicity you will undoubtedly get while you are being paid to do your job to label something and say whether you care about something or not because by wearing the rainbow armband along with you own personal message scribbled on is sending a mixed message.

Any player that does that shouldn't because they damned well know – and is that their club's view as well? The team that they are representing? Or is that their personal view? If it is, keep it to yourself until you get home where you are allowed to say it. It's quite simple, really isn't it?

One Premier League club decided not to wear Pride-themed jackets ahead of their game because a team-mate had refused to wear one because of his religious beliefs. I've heard not all the players were happy not wearing the jackets, but as a collective, that's what they decided to do. So, to make one fellah feel OK, we are all not going to support this initiative? What's wrong with him feeling OK with his team-mates deciding to make their own choice? Maybe he was OK with that – I wasn't there – but as long as he wasn't forced to something he didn't want to do; it should have been absolutely fine for the rest of his team-mates to make their own individual choices. What message does that actually send out?

Isn't it a shame we can't support inclusivity together instead of making personal stands that end up receiving much wider coverage than the actual support 99.9 of all the other players gave the show of support.

Personally, I would have worn the armband, rainbow laces or jackets because I feel that way. I feel the world is a better place when we are truly inclusive. People are raised to be a certain way, and your sexuality is something you're born with and that is inside of you – so how can that be labelled as wrong or a lifestyle choice? In some books and religions, it will be labelled as wrong because apparently God didn't believe in that – or the Gods of different religions. But hang on a minute... that's just words in a book to me. If those words in a book affect your life in a brilliant way and that's how you feel, I respect that. But you should respect me if I think something different and that's what life is about, really.

If we all liked the same thing, we'd all be queuing up outside the same girl's house because she liked one of us but not all the rest of us! What a waste of time that would be because there would be millions of us not liking each other because we all like the same thing which is that one person. I want everyone to have a good life, and I want everyone to have a slightly different better life after they've met me because I want to make them feel even better if I can.

The bottom line is we are all allowed our own opinions, and you have to be very careful in today's world how you voice them. We've seen people from this country put in prison because they've written something, but at the same time we have people writing vile racist and homophobic abuse online with total anonymity via their social media platforms who get away Scott free. They are the biggest cowards of all because they're hiding behind their keyboards. I was brought up to own what I said – and I'm not proud of everything I've ever said because I know from experience that I've said things that have then been taken and twisted into something else.

I have no prejudice, and I can't understand anyone who does – it does not compute with me to be anything else. As long as you're a good person, I don't care what you are or who you are or who you worship.

Unfortunately, people use these things to go different ways, so for me, I would wear the rainbow laces or armbands because I believe people have a right to do what they do providing it is with like-minded people and consensual. What a wonderful world that would be if we could all think and live our lives that way! We should all live in harmony, but will we ever do that? I doubt it.

AMATEUR TACTICIANS & HOW TO DEAL WITH THEM!

EVERYONE thinks they are a football manager. There can't be a manager in football who doesn't get advice on team selection, tactics and transfer targets on a daily basis from anyone and everyone. I'd been at Swindon Town for just a few weeks when I arrived at the ground on a matchday and as I got out of my car, a young lad came up to me and said, 'Are you gonna be playing three at the back again?'

I replied, 'You know what, son? I can play whatever formation I want.'

I'd had a quick glance online – not really recommended – and had seen our fans had been moaning, so it wasn't a huge surprise. I added, 'What do you know about it? I've taken over this team and only been here a few weeks, so I'm going to pick a system that suits them – because that is what they were bought for – and then I might have to change it in the January window. But in the meantime, I'm not going to play them out of position and look an absolute idiot, so do me a favour, give them a little bit more time, see how we go today and keep your opinion to yourself because I don't want to hear it, and I don't need your advice. The fewer we have at the back, the fewer mistakes they can make. Thanks ever so much.'

His mum was laughing her head off in the background. This lad has his own little blog and had been moaning about a couple of the players. He wrote about that day, 'Holloway looked nervous, I'm not so sure about him.' Then, after we'd won, it was, 'I don't know – maybe he had a point.' Or words to that effect.

Fans' negativity can get you down if you allow it to.

I remember at QPR, Paul Furlong continued to miss chance after chance and the pressure on him was becoming untenable. He failed to put a free header home in one game and did it again a couple of games later. I'd stood by him in spite of the fans' calls for him to be dropped.

He said to me, 'Don't worry Ol, I'll put them away, I've done it all my career and at least I'm getting in the right positions. I'll finish them, don't worry.'

But the pressure was beginning to tell on me and the team after his latest miss and when he said he'd start scoring, I said, 'It's about time you took responsibility, Furs, and any chance of fucking heading it in the fucking net? God isn't gonna make it go in – you should, because that's what you used to do. If you don't, I ain't gonna support you anymore. You put it where it needs to go because you're good enough.'

I'd lost it with him because I thought I was going to lose my job at any moment. Quite a large section of the Rangers fans started chanting 'Chelsea reject' at him and, bear in mind I was on a sticky wicket anyway, but I couldn't allow that and had to publicly back him.

So I did. I had a go at the boo-boys in the press conference after the game and said, 'How dare you. You ain't helping me and you're slaughtering someone because he used to play for Chelsea? How childish is that? If he's missed a couple of chances give him some stick about that – but I need you to encourage him and if anybody wants to dish out unfair stick, come round to my house in St Albans and I'll fight you on the lawn. Any chance of you lot doing your job and supporting my team? They're the ones we've got, I can't change them, let's get on with it.'

I meant it, too and felt good for saying exactly what I'd wanted to.

Another time at QPR, we were away to Plymouth Argyle at a packed Home Park, and it was during this game that some anger-management therapy I'd taken really kicked in. We were probably slightly the better team, and it was 0-0 when Mark Bircham suffered a nasty head injury. My physio went on and told me I had to bring him off because Birch was suffering from double vision, so I brought Steve Palmer on. Birch didn't want to come off and was giving me stick as he left the pitch. Our fans seemed to pick up on that because they didn't know why I'd taken him off.

So when Plymouth went ahead a few minutes later, it looked like a terrible substitution. Not long after that, they make it 2-0 and it's game over. Their fans are celebrating because that win was enough to make them the champions and it's going to be that much harder to go up automatically now.

It was a bad day all round, but it was about to get worse. On the coach going home, I get a text on my mobile from a QPR fan who hadn't put his name on the message, saying, 'Yet another inept performance, why don't you fuck off? You're ruining QPR.' His number was displayed so I called it and this guy answers.

'Who's this' he asked.

'It's Ian Holloway and you feckin' know it is, too, because my number will have displayed on your phone. Thanks for your criticism, but I actually don't agree with you because I still believe we are going to do it, but thanks for making me stronger in my belief.'

We won our last two games and were promoted back to the Championship automatically.

It used to be a case that fans would be down the pub moaning about you, and I would always avoid the local paper or nationals (depending on where I was), and it was fine. Now, there's no escape – it's everywhere – and the world is full of unnamed little trolls who are hiding behind their keyboards and are horrible. They spew out their vitriol and overall, I do my best to avoid it, but sometimes it is inescapable.

The media can be equally as bad, and they will jump on anything they can. Not so long ago, the Liverpool fans were shouting 'sacked in the morning' to Pep Guardiola for feck's sake, so he put six fingers up to them to show the amount of Premier Leagues he'd won and given the way they were with him, maybe you couldn't blame him. But in the press conference that followed, comparisons were made to when Jose Mourinho held three fingers up to the Chelsea fans giving him stick, to remind them of the titles he'd won, and Pep said, 'Yes, but I won six.'

Of course, Jose gave a pithy response at his next Fenerbahce press conference, saying how he'd won all his titles 'fairly'. Come on, man. For Christ sake keep your dignity! Pep doesn't deserve to be dragged into all of that and he doesn't need it.

He's the best manager I've ever seen and while I don't want my teams to try the same style as his – I wouldn't mind if I had the same world class players – but I appreciate how he plays because those are all his ideas.

I need my own ideas to figure out how to stop that style, because as I say, so many teams try to copy it, but very few can. You can take the ideas of someone else, but you need to add your own ideas and tweak it. And besides, Pep has never said it is a particular playing style that has worked so well for him – he's said many times, it's not about tiki-taka football at all – it's about winning the ball back inside four seconds.

And with the amount of analysis available these days, you have to continually develop your tactics and even Pep has had to do that on a regular basis and more so than ever in the 2024/25 season. Sir Alex Ferguson adapted his style many times to suit different situations, and football is like fashion and should go through many changes.

Football is all about opinions and luckily for me, I've made a living because people have paid me for mine.

So, to summarise, I think amateur tacticians are jealous because they feel they could do better, but nobody has given them a chance. That's why they're so loud and they're allowed to be loud, but I don't let it bother me, and it never will.

What does bother me is when people like Tony Pulis and Sam Allardyce – who have both had magnificent careers in management – are labelled in derogatory ways, because that doesn't make sense to me. Look at the budgets they had, the work they did with unfashionable clubs and the players they had at their disposal and the way they manufactured their teams to do what they did. It was incredible. Dave Bassett was another who worked miracles with peanuts. You have to find a way to win. . If you find a way to do that with the group you have and get them to buy into it, what a magnificent achievement that is.

Football is and always will boil down to dealing with the ball in your box, dealing with set plays from which 75% of goals come from. The game isn't being rewritten, it's just played on nicer grass, with better analysis, football science and other modern day progressions – all designed to keep the ball out of your net, win it back off them and then go up the other end and score. It can't be anything other than that and I think we'll see a renaissance of big strong centre-forwards like Erling Haaland, who hardly ever touches the ball – but when he does, he usually scores.

Everyone has an opinion and none of us are wrong – it's just some of us are employed by football clubs for our opinions – but it can be a very difficult and sometimes lonely job to have, too. That said, it's been a privilege and continues to be a privilege to do the job I love and get paid!

The only difference between a manager and a gladiator is that if the gladiator gets it wrong he dies, so I'll take being a manager over being a gladiator any day. What if you lost and it was your last ever game because you're dead? At least we get a chance to put things right, though it's not unusual for a manager to get thrown to the lions.

KEEPING PARAKEETS

I USED to have quite a big, narrow back garden about 100 metres long and on the right-hand side, I had 13 aviaries all in one line. I had maybe 13 different birds at one time, all varieties of Australian parakeets – and I used to love it. Some of them could sing, their colours were stunning and it was just wonderful.

None of them could talk, as I wouldn't have anything that could outtalk me, would I?

It teaches you about life, too. Not every egg had a baby in it, and some of the birds look exactly the same and you couldn't tell the females from the males. If you left a chick in too long with the father, he would kill it because it's his territory. I had to learn the hard way with stuff like that.

I had one bird peck another's toe off because he landed on a wire that joined two cages together and he bled to death. I didn't realise I'd infringed the bigger bird's territory because I didn't know enough about it, which was a harsh lesson for me (not to mention the poor bird).

A piece of advice for anyone thinking of keeping these

beautiful creatures is to research everything you can before you decide whether you can take on that responsibility.

At Crystal Palace, I got to see the eagle they brought in as a representative of the club's nickname and it was just incredible. What a magnificent creature and if I came back as anything, it would be an eagle for sure. You had to keep away from that thing, though. Christ, they brought him on matchdays and he was colossal – and he always looked too hungry for my liking.

No matter how long your arms were, it was never enough in my opinion, and they offered me the chance to have him on my arm on a number occasions, but I'd have needed arms that stretched out 10 feet to have agreed – no thanks. It was probably looking at me as though I was a hotdog in a suit. That beak and those talons – oh my god!

I've always loved birds and animals, and we've always had them in our family. I find their affection or occasional indifference both fascinating and therapeutic. Can you imagine just flying and soaring? Wow. Imagine how much you'd save on parking when you needed to nip into town as well? Ha!

My wife Kim has lucid dreams of flying and she is convinced her astral body leaves her physical body. I once put something in a place she couldn't reach and didn't tell her what it was. I said next time she felt herself leaving her body, to look at the object as she passed it. Next morning, she told me exactly what it was. Explain that!

So, if being an eagle would be my choice for returning to this life as a living thing, I'd have to give a wide berth to being a rat. If I were a rat, I'd know that nobody liked us, but there would be upsides, I suppose. We can climb walls; we can find our way into almost anything to make a home and we thrive on your rubbish. You hate us if we get into your garden, but we're only trying to live like everyone else. Maybe I could be like Remy, the chef rat from the Pixar movie *Ratatouille* – he was alright and was a Michelin calibre chef when all said and done. Roland Rat wasn't that popular with the kids, was he? Rats get a bad press, they really do, but apparently we're never very far away from one, so be careful what you call (us) them!

DARTS

FOR me, darts is a bit like tennis in that you have to master your mind. You'll never hit anything if you don't believe you will – you have to believe, 'I'm going to get this' and connect with your mind, otherwise it will never work.

Darts is huge today but always has been with me because I've loved it all my life. I'm never without a dartboard in our house wherever we've lived over the years. I realised early on that it's what you are thinking that helps where the dart goes and that's why Phil 'The Power' Taylor was so good.

You have to become one with what you are doing and that means endless practice, which gives you confidence to know you can hit those scores at the times you need to most. Luke Littler is proving that more than anyone – he'd just turned 18 at the time I wrote this, even though he looks 40 – but he'd already become world champion and every time he plays, he looks like he believes in every dart he throws. The amount of 180s he gets and the cockiness, for want of a better word, is unreal, just like Phil Taylor was.

All top sportsmen master their mind. I recently watched a couple of YouTube videos that came up in my suggested feed and one of them was titled 'Zidane to Modric', so I clicked on it, and it showed Zidane taking a corner, Luka Modric advancing from the middle of the half as Zidane clipped it into the space before him and Modric volleying it into the roof of the net from 25 yards. Zidane knew he could put that ball on Modric's foot and Modric knew he had the ability to hit and score first time.

It was unreal, but the thing about champions is they know they can do it and so do things without fear because they've mastered their mind, have no self-doubt and deliver when they really need to – and for me, that's what mastering darts is all about.

I think tennis is the same. The other YouTube video I watched was about Roger Federer talking to a group of school kids in America.

He told them that he'd won 80% of the tournaments he'd been in, and everyone clapped. He just smiled and then said, 'Do you know the percentage of points I won in my career? It was 54%, so how can I win 80% of the tournaments I competed in, having only won 54% of the points?'

There was silence, then he said, 'What I did was I managed to put away the bad shots and get on with the next one, better than anyone else.' It was about his mind going to the very next point and believing he could win it and that's incredible. He'd mastered his own mind and for me, this is what life is all about.

I wish I'd had the knowledge I have now when I was starting out in football because it would have been a lot easier for me. All the doubts I've lived with in my head and over my time have probably stopped me doing things, whereas now, I know I've done so many other things that I can share it with other people, and it is a joy. I've acquired data.

I play darts all the time and I'm not a bad player at all. I've hit loads of 180s, but you need practice, and I go around the board seeing how many doubles I can get, and my favourite darts game is Killer – for the record.

SCRAPPING FA CUP REPLAYS

I THINK it's terrible. The joy of the FA Cup is pitting smaller fish against bigger fish and if the smaller fish can get a draw away from home, they set themselves up for a massive payday and a match they will never forget. Take Tamworth v Tottenham in January 2025. Tamworth fight and scrap for a 0-0 draw – and probably should have won it in 90 minutes – but then have to play extra time where there was only ever going to be one winner. Spurs players are fitter, and they have big names they can bring on, so they had a lot of fresh legs and went on to win 3-0. Where's that 'FA Cup romance' in that?

Under the old rules, they draw 0-0 and then get to go and play at that magnificent Tottenham Hotspur Stadium, take maybe 6,000 fans in a crowd of 60,000 and earn half a million quid or whatever it would have been. And if the bigger teams moan, hard luck – play a stronger team and beat them first time – it's quite simple, really. I think scrapping replays is a terrible idea and if that is how it has to be, scrap extra time and go straight to penalties so at least the smaller club has an equal chance.

My first FA Cup tie as Swindon boss saw us drawn away to Accrington Stanley. We went 1-0 down then had a player sent off just before half-time. We came back to lead 2-1 before conceding in added time. So, we have 30 minutes to deal with that and were dead on our feet by the time it went to penalties, which we lost 4-1. Is that fair? It didn't feel very fair at the time.

KARAOKE

KARAOKE has been used as an initiation ceremony at a lot of clubs I've been at, but it's not something I'd really endorse as a manager. It's something the lads usually organise and if it's a tradition, it's not easy to just say, 'no, you're not doing that'. If you had a new signing, at the first away game at the hotel the night before the game and after dinner, he's got to get up on a chair and sing a song – and if you're not very good, that is horrendous. The best one ever was Kevin McLeod, who we borrowed from Everton when I was at QPR. He got up and sang Gerry Rafferty's *Stuck in the Middle* and when it came to the line, 'Clowns to the left of me, jokers to the right, here I am, stuck in the middle with you' while pointing to the staff (clowns) and then players (jokers) and it was brilliant.

Karaoke's is not always good if you're shy – but most clubs have an initiation and some of them aren't very nice, like shaving your chest, painting your nipples or god knows what else – total bullying and I don't agree with that at all. The odd song here and there by comparison isn't too bad and if you're good they'll cheer and clap you, but if you're not, you'll get booed and you'll have to sit down. Beatles or Michael Jackson songs go down well or something high in the charts at the time.

At QPR, we had Gareth Ainsworth join us and we couldn't

get him to stop! He was a singer in a band anyway, so he loved it. It was like, 'Sit down! You can only do one, you tosser!' Gareth's as good as gold, he really is and a born performer. I've never done it before but if I had to, my song would be Luther Vandross and *Never Too Much* because I know every word of that one – though that might come back to haunt me!

UFOS

UFOS or UAPs as I believe they have been recently renamed? I believe we've been lied to for years. Don't worry, this isn't a tinfoil hat moment! I just think that the governments have been covering up things for many, many years because they are scared of the reaction and think we can't handle the truth. Roswell – all of that in the New Mexico desert – I think they covered up what really happened there, and I totally believe that. There must be life on other planets and there are too many unexplained events and structures on Earth that, to me, don't stack up.

The pyramids, the huge pictures in remote territories that can only be seen from the sky – watch the movie *The Fifth Element* – that's what life's all about as far as I'm concerned. And what on Earth is going on with all the 'drones' in the US? Christ, what's all that about? We're just ants wandering about, that's all we are and there is so much more to life than we understand, but I don't need a UFO to land on my head to believe they are real – I know enough to think it is more than likely possible. And that's where I am.

Maybe, we as a race aren't ready for the truth? Maybe we don't need to know. All I know is I'm not scared, and I am ready – I'm ready to embrace all of it, if whatever 'it' is ever happens.

THE 1,000 CLUB

JUST before Christmas 2024, I took charge of my 1,000th game as a manager. It was for Swindon Town against my old club Grimsby Town, and it was a personal landmark in my career – but it's hard to see many more managers achieving that many games because of the way football has gone. Only the best of the best will get to that number in years to come because the game doesn't have the same patience that was in place when I started out at Bristol Rovers in 1996.

I was very proud to join the 1,000 Club because it's a statement that you can adapt and change, utilise the skills you've acquired in the past and tweak them for use today and I believe it's another form of data. Imagine all the info that's in my head from every situation I've ever had in football? I'm sure I'm a better brain surgeon than I used to be – and by that I mean a brain surgeon doing his first operation compared with the brain surgeon he becomes after 20 years – he's got to be that much better, and I think that can apply to many things and most certainly to football managers. So, surely after 1,000 games in management, I've got more to offer than somebody who has been doing it for five or six games? But it's a sad fact that people with data in football – or experienced managers – aren't treasured anymore.

Transfer that to players. At the time of writing, Chelsea are buying up lots of exciting young talent, but they won't learn anything without good, senior pros around them because senior pros teach younger players more than coaches do. That's a fact. In early 2025, Roy Keane said that the dressing room in his day would not have allowed Marcus Rashford and Alejandro Garnacho to not train properly at Manchester United, after various reports saying they hadn't been up to standard. He's totally right.

Everyone is obsessed with data in football these days, but you still need to collate your own and the best clubs in the world rely on themselves – they don't use someone else's info, stats and scouting. Brentford and Brighton have their own people, their own data and a trusted scouting network that continually delivers. Good luck to them because they don't make many mistakes.

It's taken me 40 years to acquire the data I have, and it's all in my head and that means that today, I can make better and well-judged decisions, more so than before. There's nothing like having that experience because it makes things much easier in your life.

On my 1,000th game, as I say, we were at home to Grimsby Town and it was ruined, really. They had a four-foot big banner – in our ground – saying I was a c**t, so how do they get in with that? I didn't make too much of it, but my lads wanted to go out there and beat them because of that, and we did, 3-1. Life's about realising that if you try your best wherever you go, what else can you do?

Things are always going out of fashion and then coming back in again – whoever thought you'd see Donald Trump back in the White House? When I think about all the managers and players I've seen in my lifetime, I wouldn't change a thing.

George Best, Sir Alex Ferguson, David Bowie, The Beatles, Elvis Presley... how lucky am I to have experienced, seen and heard all that I have in my time on this planet? I've seen some wonderful things, like man stepping on the moon for the first time – if they did? – and I wouldn't change a feckin' thing. It's been incredible and I hope there's plenty more to come.

THE MAGIC SPONGE

DID they work? Of course they didn't, but it was an almost mythical and much-loved part of yesteryear football. It was just a psychological thing and the shock of icy cold water or a spray that numbs the pain allows you to get on with it, but it was very much in the dark days of dealing with injuries. We've come a long way thank god, because a lot of those physios didn't have a clue what was going on. Telling a player, 'Go on, you'll be alright' was hardly the informed opinion of a medical expert, was it? I wonder how many lads hobbled on with ACL injuries or broken metatarsals back then?

At Bristol Rovers, we had an unqualified physio – at least as far as I'm aware – called Harold Jarman, and we had a heat lamp that had a red light on it near the top. We used that for months imagining the leaps in modern medicine were helping cure an injury. The problem was, Harold hadn't a clue how to use it properly! When a technician came to give the machine a routine maintenance check, he asked Harold, 'How long's that red light been on?'

Harold said, 'About three months.'

The guy said, 'Oh, right – well it's not been working for three months because that's the fault light.'

Ha! Imagine poor Harold's face! The thing is, we all used to feel better when we used it!

Another physio introduced a hot wax machine where you put your foot in, and it was so scalding hot it almost took all your skin off because you came out with a hot wax coating. It didn't do anything apart from give you third degree burns! It was feckin' useless! It was a horrendous time for players compared with today.

Still at Bristol Rovers, there was another guy, this time from China, who I believe was way ahead of his time. He had us doing the 'crab' – where you bend over backwards from a standing position by taking your hands over your head until they reach the ground – and by the weekend, three of us were out with back injuries caused by his methods. They got rid of him straight away, but I wish they'd kept him on.

We just weren't ready for that, or yoga and other exercises that promoted suppleness and given my playing career again, I'd be into all that massively.

We have sports science experts now, but back then, us managers had to invent our own conditioning schedules. Most of that would be based on what the lads hated, because you quickly got to know who the good characters were because they didn't moan – and the ones who did – who eventually you got rid of!

It's a bit like the army where they throw you around, treat you harshly and pick you up and it separates the ones that can deal with it all and the ones who can't. In the SAS, it's those who survive who go on to become the elite, while others steadily drop out along the way. That's life, unfortunately and in many walks, it literally is the survival of the fittest – when the going gets tough and all that. If you want your football team to be winners and pull together in times of adversity, you have to let the weaker-willed ones move on.

THROWN UNDER THE BUS

IT'S very much a reality in football that people get thrown under the bus all the time – usually managers! Someone has to take the blame and there has to be accountability, and unfortunately for managers, the buck usually stops with us. I believe I was thrown under the bus when I was in charge of Millwall. I'd kept the club up after taking over in January 2014, but we slipped into the bottom three in my first full season because we couldn't buy a goal and even though there were still two months of the season to go, I was sacked for the first time in my career. Could I have kept them up? I'll never know but their fans turned on me big style and as managers, we know we will have to take the fall because it won't be those above you. Under the bus I went!

I think the worst case of being thrown under the bus – or to the lions in this case – was David Beckham for England after the 1998 World Cup. Glenn Hoddle claimed David had been responsible for our exit and that he had let his country down – and it was horrendous because Glenn was trying to protect himself and I don't think that was right. Glenn was my hero as a player, but that was the worst example I can think of in football where somebody was hung out to dry. Thankfully, Manchester United stuck by David and he was strong enough to deal with it all. I'm sure Glenn never intended England fans to be burning effigies of David and all that nonsense, but he was the scapegoat for a nation that was once again crestfallen at a major tournament.

My advice for anyone who gets to see that underside of the bus – and it's a dark and grimy place to be – ask yourself this: what are you going to do about it? Are you going to moan and blame someone else? Or do what David Beckham did and fight through it and come out the other side stronger and more determined than ever? I'm still trying to do that now. Millwall damaged my managerial reputation, and Grimsby Town almost ended it, and I'm still trying to rebuild it. But if you are lucky, you always get a chance to prove people wrong.

OPEN-TOP BUSES

STAYING with the bus theme, in 1990 Bristol Rovers organised an open-top bus tour of the city after we won the Division 3/ League 1 title, but when it arrived to pick us up, there was a bloody brass band (including Helen Chamberlain off *Soccer AM*'s dad) sitting upstairs! We couldn't believe it – had they expected the players and our families to sit downstairs while the band played on? Only Rovers could plan an open-top bus tour with the team on the lower deck! I started moaning and got up a bit of a mutiny – mutiny on the buses if you like – and eventually they got another bus for us to go on with the band following behind. Sanity prevailed but typical Rovers! That's why I love them, I suppose.

CAMPERVANS

I'M going to keep the four-wheel theme going here and move on to my beloved campervan. Kim and I have always loved to camp with every size of tent imaginable over the years. Gradually, from a six-berth tent that could fit all the family in, they got smaller until we 'downsized' completely to a campervan, which we've found is an upgrade on tent camping by a country mile. But if you're not into camping at all, you probably won't enjoy campervans, either – it's quite simple.

My son isn't impressed and asks what on earth do we do sitting in the middle of a field using some dodgy toilet and why don't we just sit in our own front rooms in comfort? But he doesn't get it, campervans might not be to everyone's liking but we adore ours.

For us, it's more about what it represents – freedom. The freedom to go whenever you want to wherever you want is indescribably liberating and that's why we love it. We could be parked in the Scottish Highlands with a storm battering the windows and roof while you're all cosy and warm inside with your dogs on your lap, sipping tea or whatever, just listening to the elements. It's unreal. You're closer to the real world and can hear and see nature outside your window and we've done it all, really.

We had an old VW campervan; we've had a newer one – the California – and we've gone from that to something slightly bigger. There's just something about it and sometimes the worse the weather is, the better it is and in the snow, it's just magical because you can open your window and watch the snowflakes falling from the sky in silence. I compare it to being a caveman and relating to the world around you while you've got a nice fire going in your cave. Just don't make a nice fire in your campervan.

Before I returned to management at Swindon, we were in ours almost every week because I was doing after-dinner speaking around the country and we'd go to wherever the venue was, park up somewhere and I'd get a taxi to the club or whatever while Kim and the dogs stayed in the van. Kim would be doing some painting or whatever and just relaxing.

We have a little TV in there, too and you watch different shows you wouldn't normally watch because obviously you're more restricted to certain channels – just like the old days!

We play backgammon, read... stuff we don't do at home, and it feels like you're on holiday all the time – even if you're not. There's something really brilliant about it. And our dogs love it and any dog owner will tell you that if your dogs are happy and relaxed, so are you. It's quite therapeutic and relaxing.

And that freedom to be somewhere else, see different places and set off when you please is beyond comparison. It changes your life for the better. At the time of writing, our house is being renovated and there is a campsite up near our training ground in Swindon – so we might go and pitch there for a while and trust me when I say it will feel like we're on holiday! Bet there's not many managers who can claim to have been on a campsite while they managed their team, ha! Imagine Arne

Slot rocking up in his camper to stay in a field near Melwood for six weeks?

If you've never tried it, hire one out for a week and see what you're missing.

MODERN FOOTBALL BOOTS

TWO words – absolutely ridiculous. I don't like them at all and while it's great they can mould them to your feet, for me, I like tough leather and I like the tongue folded over, I like them to have laces, and I like something that feels like it will protect my foot if I am involved in a heavy challenge. I used to love the Adidas World Cup boots, the Puma King – unbelievably fantastic boots – the Predators were good, too, but I didn't like them because I didn't think I was good enough to wear them.

The new ones might leave players more susceptible to foot injuries because if you get stamped on, you could easily end up with a broken foot. I might be wrong, but who'd ever heard of metatarsal injuries before we saw these new lightweight boots? I could be wrong and maybe they are actually better for your feet – I don't want to be sued! – but I just don't like them.

I'm sure they've done a lot of research on it, and they will tell you why the boots of today are better, but I just think it's all about money (it usually is) and I just don't like it all.

I might be a bit old-fashioned in my thinking here because in my day, you had to be bloody good if you were going to wear anything other than a black pair of boots. Goddammit you would look flash in a pair of white boots back then, but if you wore them, you'd better be able to deliver the goods because you'd stand out like a sore thumb.

Plus I like the kit to match, so when I used to see Manchester United, for example, back in the late 1960s and 70s, they used to look great in their red shirts, white shorts and black socks with black boots – like a Subbuteo team!

If I see a pair of flash boots on any of my lads I always go, 'Christ, you'd better be good, son, if you're going to stand out like that!'

I've actually been put off signing a player who wears garish boots because to me, that means 'what are you trying to say about yourself, son?' It tells you an awful lot in my opinion and if you want to get some attention, just play well, don't wear some god-awful boots and a haircut to match.

CHIPPY FANS

CHIPPY football fans? Christ, they're ten-a-penny these days, aren't they? We're writing this in February 2025 and just the other week, I had chippy fans and then some away at Newport County. Some little Welsh lads – and god knows how old they were – but they were absolutely off the scale. Why kids – and adults who should know better – think they can scream and swear at you just because you're inside a football stadium and think that's absolutely fine, I have no idea. I'd love to meet some of those older ones in a pub and see if they are still as gobby, because I'd be offering them the chance to step outside if they were.

You would not believe the amount of abuse you get these days, and there are stewards standing there listening to that foul language they are using towards you, doing absolutely nothing. At Newport, all along the side where our dugouts were, they were at it all night and when they scored, I'd never heard a racket like it, banging on the back of our dugouts and creating a right old din. But in the end, they got what they deserved – nothing – because we won 2-1 – and they went away moaning at their own team instead of ours. I was laughing my head off at them. There's no respect and no need for it, but it is what it is. I don't understand why they feel the need to do it, but they do.

If they're in a group – or maybe pack is a better word – they are more likely to shout abuse, but would they do it if they were on their own? I doubt it. Would they come and say the things they say if you were out shopping in Asda? Almost certainly not. It's a mentality that is more prevalent in football than in any sport. Go to the game, enjoy it if you win and if you don't, better luck next time. Paying admission to watch a game does not give you the right to hurl abuse at another human being, you feckin' muppets!

Maybe it's always been there, but today it seems to have been elevated to 'ridiculous' level. Over what? About what? A game of football? Come on! I just don't understand why they have to moan constantly. Your ticket does not give you an entitlement to see your team win and even if you're Man City, you don't have a right to win games, you have to earn it and you, as a fan, are there for the good times and bad times. And if you've seen some good times, good luck to you. You're lucky. If you haven't, it's your choice to follow that team so put up and shut up. I don't go to any games to moan at my lads – I'm there to encourage them and you're there to support them, hence the word, 'supporter' – you're not a Liverpool moaner or a Man United moaner – you're a Liverpool supporter and a Man United supporter. A ticket does not give you the god-given right to abuse someone and when it happens, why aren't we stopping it?

I think the worst example I witnessed was when I was playing for Bristol Rovers away to Millwall. We beat them and their fans were whinging and moaning at their own players, and this one guy punched a police horse on the nose. What had the horse done to deserve that for feck's sake? Thankfully, the policeman riding the horse got out his truncheon and smacked the guy over the head, so there's justice for you. Our coach was bricked on the way out of that game – over what? It's not something I'm really that comfortable talking about if I'm honest. I'm not sure I want my grandkids to go to games when there's that threat lying around.

Will, my lad, went to the 2022 Champions League final between Real Madrid and Liverpool. I'd managed to get him and his mate two tickets for the game in Paris and he said it was the most frightening experience of his life. There were gangs mugging people everywhere, the police were horrendous and treated the fans like animals and he was separated from the people he was with by force. His ticket came up as not valid – it was – and by the time he got into the stadium, all he wanted to do was go home. How can that happen at a showpiece event like that?

I enjoy the sporting banter, but where's that gone? That's what I grew up with – an attitude that if you got beat, there's not much you can do about it, so you accept it, shake hands and off you go. That's how it should be, surely? Not gesticulating 'wanker' hand movements, hurling insults and taking the piss out of the opposition players and fans. I just don't get it. Deary me. It's all bullshit and absolute nonsense and if you want to fight, get in a boxing ring and channel your aggression into a sport designed for direct combat.

It's just a sad reflection of the world today, and it's not how I want it to be and for me, I'd get anyone who was caught hurling abuse, personal or otherwise, banned from football grounds for the rest of their lives.

It's just something about football and tribalism – you don't see people at Wimbledon get up when Roger Federer is walking towards them between points getting up and shouting, 'Federer you wanker!' Can you imagine? They'd be ejected in the blink of an eye!

IAN HOLLOWAY

If only some of the more unsavoury football fans could be like the darts fans at the Ally Pally every Christmas. They might have their favourites, but they're there to enjoy the occasion, appreciate the skill and come in fancy dress, singing non-stop and getting drunk but just having a good time. It can be done.

It's a wonderful, safe atmosphere and I think we should take a leaf out of their book, though the ironic thing is, the majority who attend probably also go to football matches and some will act ridiculously.

So, chippy fans? I was going to say don't get me started, but I think I've finished now...

PODCASTS

I LOVE them. You can listen to them anytime, anywhere and in any situation. You could be on a long drive, in the bath, on the bus, in the garden, recovering from illness or whatever and there are literally thousands of them to go at. They are great entertainment but also a fantastic educational tool to increase your knowledge.

I'm not a prolific reader, so for me, it's a wonderful and interesting way to acquire information. You can get a podcast about absolutely anything and it's mostly free, too, so I can only see them becoming more and more popular because people will always sit and listen.

Kim and I enjoy *Undr the Cosh* – the football podcast with Jon Parkin, Chris Brown and t'other one – it's really good, full of great footy banter and great guests and I enjoy listening to them because they are so relatable. Parky and company are doing a great job.

We also like *The Joe Rogan Experience* and the way he is on his show – he's quite brutal with all his guests, but it makes for a great listen.

I've toyed with doing one in the future and if people found it interesting, I'd give it a good go I reckon. I had planned to do a series of interviews in our campervan, travelling around meeting different personalities, but we'll see what happens further down the line.

YouTube is another great form of entertainment and something we watch regularly. We like shows of all kinds – maybe people who have no home, but are just living out of their campervan, or they might have bought an old van and converted it into something they can live in and it's all insanely brilliant! Then there are guys who go stealth camping on roundabouts where you're not supposed to. There's a bloke who just goes and sits in the woods in America, another guy who eats nothing but hot noodles! There are paranormal shows where nothing much ever happens – also known in our house as 'Nothing Happens TV' – anything and everything and a lot of them get millions of views.

I also love audiobooks, and I remember driving around the Scottish Highlands listening to Kenny Dalglish's autobiography some years back. Trust me, if you are driving around Scotland, it doesn't get any better than listening to Kenny talk about his life and career. Whenever I hear his voice now, I'm taken back to that magical trip through the Scottish glens, narrated by one of the game's greatest players.

That's what is so wonderful about your mind. You can hear sounds, smells, music or whatever and be reminded of a special moment in your life. Kim and I had Rose Royce playing at our wedding, so whenever we hear her, we are transported back to that day each and every time. How good is that? For me, the more things you have like that, the better and more enriched your life is.

FIVE-A-SIDE

I DON'T like five-a-side. It has to be six-a-side for me, with one goalie and five outfield players, otherwise you have a keeper, two in defence and two in midfield with nobody up top, which is something you should never have. So six is the minimum you should ever have and for me, just having five is garbage.

I use small-sided games in training, but never less than six. I didn't play it that much in my career as they usually wanted me on a bigger pitch so I could improve my running. As I was a box-to-box midfielder, they wanted me to focus on the real area I would be operating in rather than a limited sized pitch.

It was position-specific training, and it helped me out a lot and that sort of made me who I am, because I now understand where you are on a pitch and what's required of you. So, I can replicate that on a bigger pitch and take them to their specific area of the pitch they play in – be that full-back, centre-back or whatever – and demonstrate exactly what I'm trying to explain because it's totally relevant to them.

No manager of mine loved five-a-side more than Gerry Francis. On the Monday at training, we'd go over whatever we'd gotten wrong on the previous Saturday and then end with a five-a-side tournament. We might have had three teams with one waiting to come on, but there was one rule – Gerry's team had to win, no matter what! We'd keep going and keep going until he won and sometimes it would get pretty dark. You always knew that if you wanted to get home on time for tea, you had to let Gerry's team win.

He'd use that as a reward and you could learn some good habits from it, too.

Occasionally, I'll do demos on the pitch to explain what I'm looking for. I think it will help, but I can't play anymore because the twisting and turning doesn't do you any favours at my age! If I tried, I'd be staggering all over the place like a boxer who'd taken an uppercut. Maybe I should try walking football, though I just reckon they're a load of cheats! Are you telling me players don't accelerate on occasion? Ha! I do miss playing and when people ask me which I enjoyed, playing or managing, it was playing all the time.

STUBBORN MANAGER PHILOSOPHIES

IT'S become very topical to discuss what is best described as 'stubborn manager philosophies'. Managers who steadfastly stick by their principles no matter what and in 2024/25, Ruben Amorim and Ange Postecoglou (who I praised in an earlier chapter!) were firmly under the microscope.

All I would say, is that it is nice if you are given the time to implement your style and get everyone to change to your way of thinking, because time is a rare commodity in today's game, with managers getting less time than ever before in general. Look at Sir Alex Ferguson. Manchester United were patient with him because there were a number of occasions they could have sacked him, but he was allowed to build about four or five sides, and did they all play the same way? No. He adapted his style, made tweaks and didn't do too badly, did he?

I've always had to adapt to the players I've inherited to stay in a job. So, it's alright having success in certain areas, but you have to learn other things as you go along, and I'll always think the best managers are the ones who can adapt. They are certainly the ones who get what most managers crave – longevity!

Pep Guardiola has adapted since he arrived at Manchester City. He's got a goalkeeper that can kick it a mile to feet, so his team doesn't always play out from the back and occasionally, they go over the top, miss the press out completely and are on the attack. You have to keep evolving and trying to keep one step ahead.

Whether Amorim or Big Ange decide to change because they feel they're running out of time, we'll have to wait and see. Maybe they won't, maybe their way will bring success, and they can stick two fingers up at everyone else. Unfortunately, football is all about recruitment and if you inherit a different shape to the one you want to use, and still use the same players you've inherited, I don't think it works.

At Crystal Palace, I tried to play another way to the one the players there were used to, but I had to revert to how they played before to get them promoted, because my way wasn't working, and it was the old way that suited them best. When we did go up, I tried to change things again and I think I lasted eight or nine games before they got rid of me because they couldn't do what I wanted them to do and I hadn't enjoyed the way they played before. I think the three or four managers after me had the same problem before they gave it to Tony Pulis who kept them up playing in a style they were most effective.

MOTORWAY SERVICES

I CAN'T believe motorway services get away with charging as much as they do for anything and everything. Unless you're a lorry driver who gets a discount, how can anyone afford to eat anything at these places? I think the best one is Gloucester which has a farm shop serving beautiful, fresh, healthy food. It has a lake, and a grass-covered roof and it's just wonderful. You can still spend a fortune in there, but the food is first class, and it feels more like a holiday destination! Most of the others – apart from Tebay on the M6 North – charge ridiculous prices for everything and how unhealthy is most of the food?

People don't really have a choice, do they? They have to stop at some stage and if they have kids, they'll probably want McDonald's or KFC. You end up paying the equivalent of a week's shopping if you do stop and eat.

When I was at Plymouth, we stopped at a lot of motorway services and got to know them all pretty well because everywhere was a long trek. The journeys could vary in enjoyment. It often depended on what other fans were travelling at the same time and how we got on.

If you've won, it can be really nice because you'll see your own fans and they'll be made up and happy to see you – not so much if you've lost!

We did have to stop off because the coach driver needs a 45-minute break, but it can be difficult to watch what the lads are eating if you've got 20 of them spread around the building. At Blackpool, Gary Taylor-Fletcher only had to walk past the sweets counter of WHSmiths to put a few pounds of weight on.

You have to keep your eye on one or two, that's for sure and if they get a coffee, make sure that they've not picked up a huge muffin or packet of biscuits to accompany it. We do have food on the coach, but if we have to stop, I'm always on high alert.

When I was doing the after-dinner circuit between management jobs, almost every interaction with football fans at services was really nice and pleasant because I wasn't linked with another club. As I say, when you're back in, that tribalism can come to the forefront again.

MOST EMBARRASSING MOMENT

THIS is so bad. And my most embarrassing moment in football wasn't on the pitch, and it wasn't in the dugout – it came during my media career when I was on air with Quest TV's Football League show with Colin Murray. I was a guest on a morning show, but I had a really bad stomach and felt ill – I think it was food poisoning – so eventually, I had to make a dash to the toilet. That was OK, but I hadn't taken my lapel microphone off and you can probably see where this is going...

I dashed for the loo, with no knowledge my mic was still on and they could hear everything as I pebble-dashed the toilet basin, groaning and moaning as I let rip and blew toxic gas out of my arse. It was horrendous and I was crying out in pain, all while 20 people listened to my every (bowel) movement. I knew what had happened the moment I came out because it was then I saw the red light on my mic device! Christ, no! Ha! How bad is that? The next time I saw them, it was, 'Oh, here he is. Mr arrghh! Woooah! Jesus!' followed by wind-breaking sounds. A few of them say they still can't sleep...

The worst thing I ever did as a manager was captured by a photographer for eternity and I still look at the picture and think, 'Christ, what was I thinking?' It was while I was at QPR, and we were getting all kinds of dog's abuse at the time from our fans.

It was at Loftus Road in 2002, and we were 1-0 down to Brentford and most of our supporters had left, but we ended up scoring in the last minute to get a 1-1 draw. I went absolutely mental at their bench and their manager Dean Smith, who I really like. I pulled the worst face you've ever seen – I still have the picture which is included in this book, and it was just a horrible, horrible moment and I wish I'd never done it. Sorry, Dean. I then had a right go at our fans in the post-match press conference for having such a pop at us during the game and because so many of them had left early.

Again at QPR, there was a moment when I faced some direct abuse from a supporter, but this time I think I handled it pretty well.

I'd like to think that at least 95% of this book is original for readers who have bought my first two books – probably more than 95% – but occasionally, forgive me for throwing in a 'golden oldie!' This particular snippet appeared in my 2007 autobiography *Ollie* and is all about taking the fire out of the moment with a decent comeback.

We were going through a pretty bad patch of form but were drawing 0-0 with Cardiff City and just about holding firm with an hour gone. We ended up losing 4-0 after collapsing like a pack of cards as Rob Earnshaw scored a hat-trick inside 28 minutes. I'm stood there watching all this in my technical area as a woman comes from nowhere – she must have climbed over the small perimeter wall at Loftus Road and came from my right. As she approached, I thought back to a few nights before when I'd spoken with my wife Kim about handling any personal abuse that might come my way, and she just said, 'Why don't you just reply, 'I'm all of that plus a bag of chips.' It'll diffuse any situation.' God bless her for that! It made me laugh, so I rehearsed it at home and this woman is now right up to me and she says, 'You're a fucking wanker, Holloway!' and then threw her season-ticket at me. I just looked at her and said, 'I tell you what love, I'm all that and a bag of chips.'

She didn't know what to add to that, threw her season-ticket book at me and a couple of stewards helped escort her away. I looked back at my bench who were smiling at what I'd said, but I was just pleased I had a decent comeback. It wasn't very nice to have that from one of your own fans, but unfortunately you get used to it. I picked up her season-ticket book and it was bloody empty! She must have taken all the tickets for the rest of the season out and wanted to throw it as a public act of disgust.

As recently as December 2024, my Swindon Town team went to Colchester United and by 38 minutes, we were 4-0 down. I looked at my bench and everyone's shoulders were down, my players looked beaten, and we still had maybe 60 minutes to play. That was an embarrassing and bad moment, but it's not about how it was, it's about what you can do to get over it and make things better. How can you respond? And that's what keeps me going and there are times I have to pick myself up, encourage myself and get going again.

So, in life, when you face adversity, my advice would be this: that was then, this is now and with the right attitude and belief, you can change anything. You can change your outcomes if you believe you can. And a bag of chips can have many uses!

THE AFTER-DINNER CIRCUIT & SPEECHES

THIS is something I've been doing for quite a while and it's wonderful. It's quite something to be able to stand there, share stories and offer advice to so many people who actually want to listen to what you want to say.

I always have a fear as I drive to these events that I'll be the only one up on stage, holding a mic in front of an empty room because nobody could be bothered to buy a ticket. When I get there, the first thing I try to do is read the room.

I always listen to the comedians first and you can learn a lot from them because they are very serious people away from the stage. If they can't make people laugh, it absolutely slaughters them in their brain, and they're left wondering what they do next. It's such a difficult way to earn a living.

I just tell the stories I know in a slightly different way each time, tweaking or adapting them to the audience I'm talking to, and learning as I go. It amazes me so many people come out to listen to the nonsense I occasionally spout and I absolutely love doing it.

As anyone who knows me will attest, I've never had a problem talking! I didn't like studying at school much, but if I could go up and talk for whatever reason, I was in my element and I carried that on into my career, as any journalist who ever attended one of my press conferences will confirm! I like a good speech, and I could talk for England. As a manager, you get used to talking a lot and trying to evoke some emotion, reaction or trying to inspire your players. You get used to it and I've had such a wonderful life that I've collected a lot of stories along the way, many of which I've found quite funny because it's also important you don't take yourself too seriously.

I try to inspire my players and there is one standout moment where I felt I got it just about right.

It was in my QPR days as a manager and our season was all on the final game against Sheffield Wednesday at Hillsborough. Win and we were going up, but the tension was palpable among the lads, and I needed to come up with something special. I'd already decided I was going to tell the lads how well they'd done regardless of whether we went up or not, but I was struggling for something to say ahead of the game, so I decided to dig out my old Bristol Rovers Division Three champions medal and put it in my top pocket.

It's always difficult to know what to say in a pressure situation like that, but I had an idea and just before we got on the coach at our Sheffield hotel, we were waiting in the reception among quite a few Rangers fans who were coming up and wishing us luck. I sat down with our lads and invited the fans to come and sit with us as I did what I hoped would be my pep talk.

Steve Palmer had asked if I thought it would be OK because the fans were there, and I just told him not to worry because I knew what I was doing. We'd been over our tactics in training so this was purely aimed at getting something in their hearts and minds that might just edge things our way. So the lads and some of the Rangers fans were all sat around in front of me, and I began. I said, 'I've had some special times in my life and it was the people I was with at Bristol Rovers that helped me win this medal – my teammates. I don't know if we're going to get promoted today, but I just wanted you to hear what these supporters think of you regardless of what happens.'

I asked a young kid to step up and say something to the lads and he smiled, took a deep breath and said, 'You've been brilliant! Absolutely brilliant!' I asked another bloke to step up and he said how proud he was of how hard we'd battled. I then said, 'As long as we come off that pitch today and we couldn't have done any more, I won't have a problem. I've cherished this medal all my life, and I hope you have the chance to cherish something with a group of people because for me, you've earned the right to do that, and you couldn't fail me if you tried today because you're already a success.' It was emotional stuff, I admit, and I had no idea whether it would help or not. It hadn't been about football, it had been about people, and I wanted them to understand how everyone felt, no matter what.

So we start the game and after 10 minutes their scoreboard flashes up that Bristol City are 1-0 up, which meant if they won and we didn't, they would go up instead of us. I couldn't believe it and felt it was absolutely scandalous to do that while my lads were still playing. I couldn't give a monkey's what happened at half-time, but that wasn't right. Then, a few minutes later, it flashed up that Bristol City are 2-0 up, so as it stands, we're not going up automatically.

I got up and told Steve Palmer to calm everyone down and it took another 10 minutes for us to stop wobbling. Their fans were singing that we weren't going up and I was fuming inside, though outwardly calm. Then, finally, Kevin Gallen puts us 1-0 up and my lot finally settle down. There wasn't much that needed saying at the break and in the second half Paul Furlong, born again bad by that time, makes it 2-0 – but Wednesday pull one back and we're all on pins again.

That's when I went into slow-motion mode and when I get nervous I need the toilet, so I end up going back and forth three times in the last 10 minutes. Just as I go back out for the last time, Martin Rowlands hits a ball across and it takes a deflection, wrongfoots the keeper and we go 3-1 up. Time seemed to go backwards, and I thought there were still a few minutes left when my keeper coach Tony Roberts grabs me and I tell him to get off because it's not finished. He says, 'We've done it! He's gonna blow any second!' And then he grabs me again because the ref actually blew and four or five others joined in, jumping on top.

I'd been told by officials we had to get back in the tunnel in case of a pitch invasion so, still in some kind of weird mental haze or disbelief and denial, I break free and trot down towards the dressing rooms and as I do, I glance up at a scoreboard that says: 'Owls 1, QPR 3' and it starts to sink in. I couldn't believe it. We pipped Bristol City by a point and their manager Danny Wilson called me up to say well done – and shortly after he gets the sack.

So, I guess I'm well suited to the after-dinner circuit because I'm lucky in that everything that's ever happened in my career is still crystal-clear, and I enjoy sharing my experiences with people – I guess that also applies to a lot of this book. It's just bits and pieces I've gathered along the way that I hope you're enjoying.

I've hardly ever had a bad night on the circuit, if I'm honest and I like to think I can read people well and can change where I'm going quickly if the situation needs it. And the funny thing is, I think I'm a better football manager because I've done the after-dinner stuff so many times over the years. I've learned such a lot, and I can now sift through what I might have said before and condense it down more succinctly because I believe I know what works and what doesn't.

As long as you end up making your audience think, you've had a good night because as a football manager, I think we affect everybody's life in some way or another.

At these events, I often work with people who are under pressure to work well for other people, and just because they are good at what they do, it doesn't mean they are getting the results they want. My message is getting away from a blaming culture because it is so destructive. It's about being resilient, helping each other through ups and downs and that's what life is about.

So the messages I try to send out to businesses, corporate clients or whatever, is also what I am telling my lads each week, because the same applies in sport as it does in other walks of life. Being on the road has helped me understand that.

I've done talks at schools, for the army, the SAS and it's been an absolute privilege.

I must have done hundreds and hundreds over the course of my life and one of my favourites was for our future king, Prince William. When I was manager at Blackpool, we were at home to Aston Villa and my CEO Matt Williams came up and asked whether I'd do a speech for Prince William, who was having a do in a couple of private boxes at Bloomfield Road. He's obviously a Villa fan and I was more than happy to go up and say a few words before he headed out on a friend's stag do in Blackpool.

I did a pre-match talk sort of speech to His Royal Highness

and said, 'Leave our women alone, because most of them are men and he might get a nasty surprise.' It actually went down a storm, and I mentioned that I loved his mum and to tell his dad to stop talking to plants. Harry near fell off his chair – that was before they fell out – but what a privilege and how lucky was I?

I REALLY DID LIKE TO BE BESIDE THE SEASIDE...

I WILL always look back on my time as Blackpool manager as one of the happiest times of my football career. People often ask me what it was like living in the town. I always used to say that Blackpool and I had a lot in common in that we both looked better in the dark, but the truth is I have a lot of affection for the place and always will.

Getting Blackpool to the Premier League was fantastic for the club, fantastic for the players and fans and wonderful for me and the town itself. Sky loved the fact that this saucy seaside postcard club were rubbing shoulders with the big boys, and they couldn't get enough of us for that one, unforgettable season in the Premier League.

The general media had predicted we would be the worst team in the history of the division – quite a statement given Derby County's 11-point campaign of 2007/08, but my lads and I loved that. If we hadn't had fire in our bellies, we would have never got there in the first place but what was being said about us lit an inferno. I never doubted we would give it a right good go – and boy, we almost pulled it off – but more about that in a bit.

What my team did for Blackpool was put it back in the hearts and minds of the nation. We were a free advert for everything Blackpool had to offer and the 2010/11 season was worth an estimated £25m worth of publicity – that was the price they put on what it would have cost to get the same sort of exposure through a TV and media campaign.

Plus, there were 3,000 or more travelling fans coming to Bloomfield Road every other week, and a large number of those would stay over for the weekend. That could equate to maybe 50,000 additional visitors staying, eating and having fun in Blackpool and you can work out the average spend on that yourselves! But you get the picture. I'm not saying we invented tourism or even that we reinvented it, but we gave it a decent shot in the arm, and I just wish that could have continued longer than it did.

Initially, Kim and I tried to live in Blackpool for a while, but it became impossible. We literally couldn't go anywhere without being stopped and as much as we loved it, we needed our own space to breathe and so we ended up going to Pendle near Burnley. Pendle Hill is where 10 people – mostly women – were hung at trials in 1612 after being found guilty of practising witchcraft. So, basically, they were murdered.

Of course, Kim chose the house we rented and the first thing she said when we arrived at Pendle Hill was, 'I can't believe I'm back here'. Ha! That's Mrs Holloway! And she meant it, too!

Blackpool is a great place, full of fun and it's very much a summer town because that biting wind off the Irish Sea in the winter months is horrendous. The wind used to blow our training pitch goals sideways, you got sandblasted regularly from the gusts coming across the beach and some days we just couldn't train.

But it was wonderful, too, in its own way. Getting down to the beach on a frosty morning for a run and you could feel the history of our former greats who would have done the same thing all those years ago – we were literally following the footsteps of such legends as Sir Stanley Matthews and Stan Mortensen, and that is a very inspiring feeling.

I'd take the lads down and I'd tell them, 'Come on, this is our heritage.' We went to the Pleasure Beach on another occasion with my players and we all went on the Big One, which was a bit rickety if I'm honest – I've never been on it since! But we were celebrating the town, its history and all it had to offer to intertwine ourselves with its DNA.

It was amazing and absolutely fantastic, and I know why we played in orange – because everything that can rust in Blackpool does rust and turns a sort of orangey colour – thanks to the wind, rain and salt water off the Irish Sea.

That season, we went into the final day as one of three or four clubs that could stay in the Premier League. Our only problem was that we had Manchester United at Old Trafford! They were already Premier League champions, and with 62 minutes gone in that game, we were winning 2-1. Then Anderson levelled, Michael Owen came on, Ian Evatt scored an own goal and Owen got another to give United a 4-2 win.

Over the season, the problem for us was we conceded too many goals in the last 20 minutes of games. For instance, with 72 minutes played, we were beating United 2-0 at our place earlier in the season, and we ended up losing 3-2 because Fergie could bring on players like Ryan Giggs and Javier Hernandez. We were holding Man City 1-1 with 78 minutes played but

Roberto Mancini could bring on David Silva and Patrick Vieira and we lost 3-2 – and there were numerous other examples. We were coming up against teams who could bring on one, two or three superstars to change the trajectory of the game. We just couldn't compete against that sort of quality coming on late in the game, especially with the size of the squad and our budget.

We came so close, but other results went against us, and we were relegated with 39 points – one point and three goals short of survival. That 40-point mark is not a myth! Our 55 goals scored was the same as fifth-placed Tottenham, so we went down knowing we'd entertained everyone, given it a good go and I guess if any club is going to have a roller coaster season, it's Blackpool Football Club! We gave it our best, and I know the fans and the lads I had still talk about it – in fact, all my players still have a WhatsApp group to this day, some 15 years later. If that's not an example of the team spirit and camaraderie we had, I don't know what is.

As a footnote to this entry, we managed to make the Championship play-off final the following season, conceding a couple of minutes from time against West Ham to lose 2-1 in front of almost 80,000 people.

As with many things in football, it all ended in tears and turned a bit sour because the supporters weren't happy with Karl Oyston. Not many people get to leave on top in the way Sir Alex Ferguson did at Manchester United. But nobody can take away my time with Blackpool.

BECOMING A GRANDPARENT

I THINK it had to be the proudest moment of my life.

Holding your offspring's offspring is something else and everyone who has been fortunate enough to experience it will know exactly what I'm on about, because it makes you realise why you're here.

And it's brilliant, too, because at the end of the day, you can give them back! Grandparents have that extra time to spend with them and spoil them, maybe when you didn't have that with your own, and you get to build special relationships and do stuff with them.

You can help make them feel important and as long as you're aligning with their parents and what they are trying to do, you won't steer them too far off the beaten track. It's like having a separate bank account where you can put some savings into because you're investing in them.

It's hugely rewarding, watching their eyes light up over the simplest of things and helps you appreciate stuff in a different ways. Getting to know who they are and who they are going to become. You see their personalities evolve, which is a joy –

because they are all completely different – it's just a wonderful and indescribable feeling.

You're their back-up, an overseeing presence and guidance, but they can also make you feel guilty when you realise that you perhaps didn't give enough time to your own kids, so it's a special, special thing that has made Kim and I feel complete.

You have to teach them and help mould them, too. You're trying to help your own kids by helping their kids become the people they aspire to be. Each generation is different, so you have to be flexible and move with the times. And you have to find your grandkids' currency – what motivates them and gets their interest, and if they're not good, they don't get rewarded.

One of ours asked for a birthday present just before their birthday and was pretty insistent about it, so we got them nothing, because asking for one, we explained, is rude. They asked, asked, asked... we told them the rules, but they kept on asking what we were buying them, and so they ended up with nothing. We only give presents to those who deserve them! The sooner you get your life lessons and ground rules in place, the better.

We have eight grandchildren and a cuckoo – a 'grandcubby' we've inherited and adopted from somebody else's nest! Nine in total and it's just brilliant because they make you laugh out loud, occcasionally you have to bite your lip to stop laughing at the things they do or say and sometimes – quite often, in fact – there are tears and tantrums.

I love asking them about school and about what they learned that day, and they always come back with something. I tell them that they should be very proud if they can understand what the teacher says and then they can come home and tell me.

We take them places we wouldn't normally go. We went to

Bristol Zoo one time, and I tried my best to have them kept there! Visit the wolves pen or whatever, but the zookeeper wasn't having it.

They loved the snake pit and there was a black mamba with a sign that said, 'this snake has killed six people in a village' and I was looking at it thinking, 'can snakes bite through toughened glass?' It's the stuff of nightmares, isn't it? But the grandkids loved it!

They were like, 'Wow! Gramps, imagine that? Six people!'

Reading to them at night if they stay over – they love that, and so do I. I could honestly fill three chapters with the adventures we've had with our lot, but I'll move on now, save to say it's one of the most wonderful things in life having grandkids, building your relationships with them and just enjoying their company.

OUIJA BOARDS

SOMETHING I would absolutely never do is use one of these things. I wouldn't dare delve into something I didn't understand because I think there are other realms that exist that I really don't want to get involved in. I wouldn't want to be followed or give the opportunity for something to attach themselves to me that could be quite nasty.

Kim has shown me far too many things – enough for me to be convinced that using one of those things would not be a good idea. We've watched hours and hours of paranormal shows on TV – the ones where a small team armed with cameras, voice boxes and god knows what else go ghost-hunting in old, abandoned buildings and you never really see anything other than a few dust mites through a night vision camera or the odd thing that goes bump off camera.

So, would I muck about with something I didn't know much about or completely understand like a Ouija board? No chance. If there was another realm, would I want to unlock it into our world? Absolutely not. So you won't ever find me mucking about with that nonsense. Kim's the same.

We've been to see performers and magicians, but never one with a Ouija board. I'd stay right away from all that. Don't mess with things you don't know because the risk is too great.

FLYING

SOMEONE asked me once, 'Are you scared of flying?' and I said, 'No. But I am scared of crashing.' You have to get around if you're in football and it's a fantastic way to travel because more often than not, you're up and then you're down at a speed you could never match on the ground.

It allows you to see the world and some wonderful places. I would hate to get a car, boat and a train to get somewhere overseas, so I'm all for it. Kim doesn't particularly enjoy it, and she almost rips my hand off on take-off or landing, but I find taking off exhilarating. Taking the grandkids with you is great because they just see it as an adventure.

We've had a couple of bad flights and diverted journeys, but nothing too scary. At Plymouth, we once chartered a plane to Sunderland and travelled with some of our supporters and that was a fantastic experience, most likely because we won. I'd have probably still been on the coach today if we'd gone by road, and that was 14 years ago!

ROAD RAGE

I USED to have this, big time, but now 'traffic is my friend'! Kim didn't like who I became behind the steering wheel and helped me change my ways, because when you realise you're just being a selfish git who believes in your own self-importance – such as you are in a rush, so everyone else should get out of your way – you understand why getting irate in traffic is completely pointless.

Kim showed me an article that was designed to highlight why having road rage does absolutely nothing other than raise your blood pressure. It pointed out that, if you look at the situation differently, you can deal with it in a completely calm, serene way. It said something along the lines of, *if you are stuck in traffic, you can relax, and you aren't having to go fast and risk your life. Use the time to have a think, contemplate and consider things. Sitting there steaming doesn't make one iota of difference and you would only upset everyone else, so the answer is to treat traffic as your friend!*

It's hilarious I know, but I literally say to myself when I hit a traffic jam, 'traffic is my friend', or 'I love the M25'. Laugh all you like, but it feckin' works! The moral is, thinking you're more important than everyone else is beyond arrogant and if you haven't allowed enough time to get to where you need to be by factoring in possible delays, well you're a chicken nugget anyway, aren't you? Life is too fast and while you might feel like you're wasting precious time, actually you are safe. Just enjoy the moment and think about something more pleasant.

TIMEWASTING

THIS is something I can't stand and have never encouraged any of my teams to do – and never will. I always want to get on and score the next goal – that's just the way I've always thought and I'm not going to change now.

In my first season at Swindon, we came up against a team who tried everything they could to get across the line when they were 1-0 up, but they ran out of time because we beat them with three late goals – two scored in the added time they'd caused by wasting so much of it during the feckin' game! Take that! I call it poetic justice.

Their players were rolling about on the floor, feigning injury, taking an age to take throw-ins, goal-kicks or whatever and using every delaying tactic they could come up with, but the ref saw right through it. After we equalised, just before the end of normal time, he added on the time they'd wasted, and we scored another two goals to win the game.

I asked their manager afterwards what they'd been playing at, and he said, 'You've got to do what you can to try and win'. I said, 'Try to win? How's that trying to win? You want to try and score another goal instead of hanging on to what you've got. Christ, man!' To me, it's another form of cheating so you don't get beat and what's the point of doing that? It frustrates the hell out of me, and I thought I might have calmed down by now, but when I see it happening, I get as angry as I ever did.

GOLF

WHAT can I say about golf, other than it ruins a lovely walk? I've realised where I've been going wrong with golf – the ball is too close to my feet – unfortunately, that's after I've hit it. I can hit one decent shot and the next 30 are crap, and by the time I've lost my temper and thought I should be better than that, I'm usually headed back to the pavilion.

It looks crazily easy and it's just mingingly hard. And if you play against someone who is better than you – pretty much everyone I play against in my case – you absolutely despise them by the end of the round because they make it look so easy.

I was playing against my lovely wife, and she chipped one straight in the hole from off the green and said, 'Oh, look – it's gone straight in' and I was like, 'Jesus Christ – how could you?' She had no etiquette and was laughing her head off at me because I was teaching her how to play and she was already better than me. It was embarrassing.

I've had lessons with a professional that have made me worse! I just can't get to grips with it, no matter what, but it's a great sport, I love to watch it on TV and have nothing but admiration for top professionals because I understand their skill and I appreciate what they can do. One day I will go to a major and

151

see these guys up close and watch in awe and say, 'Christ I wish I could do that – but I can't!' But as far as me playing and trying to get better at it? Nah – I'll stick to darts.

ART

PEOPLE tell me I'm not bad at painting, but I've not got a clue why I can paint or why people seem to like what I do. I've had no formal training as such, and I suppose I started when I was a kid, picking up a pencil off the sideboard and doodling from a very young age. Mum would be talking in the background, and I'd just be idly scribbling on a pad and as time went on, I'd attempt to draw more specific things.

I found I had trouble just sitting down, doing nothing and would be fidgety and feel the need to do something – I think some people would call some of the traits I had either OCD or maybe even ADHD – maybe it was, I don't know. I never thought I was particularly good, but as time went on, I began doing portraits of people I liked or admired.

I never believed you had to be particularly good to do art – in my opinion, art is something that is evocative and elicits a reaction. I think we've all seen expensive works of art that look like a few splashes of paint on a canvas. Probably no two people will see art the same way, and that's something I love about it. It can reach deep inside you and bring out a feeling or appreciation maybe you never even realised you had, and you might not even understand exactly why you like something. How can that be a bad thing?

You are either into it, or you're not.

You could argue art first began with cavemen, with their efforts found inside caves thousands of years later. Art on canvas probably started because people wanted to record likenesses or landscapes because they couldn't take photographs yet, and I've always found that amazing.

If you want to paint something you love and can capture it on canvas, it's there forever and that's something I cherish. You might capture a moment in time, an expression, or art can be a depiction of who somebody is if you have the talent – a particular look that captures their very essence or even humanity.

Once you get into the light you can capture in art, you are elevated to another level. You have to ask where the light in the picture, drawing or painting is actually coming from and what effect is it having? Where is the source, what's it reflecting on and what shadows is it making? When you get into it, it's so goddamned interesting.

Kim and I had art lessons with an expert in Corsham and the first thing he said to us was, 'I can't make you better artists, but I can make you see more.' He made us draw these matchboxes he dropped all over the table and asked us where the shadows were and where the light was coming from. It was so incredible and interesting.

I love art and I love all different types of art. It's been there all my life – and the more you draw and the more you paint, the more you see through an appreciative eye. That guy was right – he taught us to see things differently and it was just wonderful.

And you know what? Anyone can do it and there is something completely liberating about getting some paint, having a blank canvas and going bob, bob, bob and creating something you've come up with. Incredible.

My favourite is a portrait of a girl with a pearl earring. I saw

Banksy version on a wall in Bristol and the earring was the building's outside alarm on the wall. Just brilliant and beautiful, so I did something similar that now sits in my living room.

Of course, I've done some of my favourite people in football, too. I did one of Georgie Best, which I gave to the SAS to raffle off. I've done two of Kenny Dalglish plus ones of Jurgen Klopp, Pep Guardiola, Steven Gerrard, Paolo Di Canio and more recently I've done a few family portraits – I've been doing them for years.

If you've never touched a paintbrush since being a kid, give it a go – I can't recommend its therapeutic benefits highly enough.

CHARITY SHOPS

TALKING of therapy sessions, how about charity shops? You can't keep me out of them! Kim and I love them, and we spend hours wandering around them. The prices are amazing, and some people might think it's pretty sad, but I think I'm addicted because you never know what you're going to find. I don't know why I'm still looking, given all the stuff we've bought over the years, but I think it's something we're always going to do. We love knick-knackery and going around flea markets, but charity shops are just banging, and we can't get enough of them.

I can't say what my best find has been because there's been too many. But among my favourites was a tweed jacket that I had for 15 years before the moths ate it. We had a moth infestation in our last house, I hadn't worn it for a few months and when I got it out to put it on, it was covered in holes the size of golf balls. I was gutted.

It was from Lyme Regis, and I always imagine what the backstory might have been to how it ended up there. Maybe it was from an old fella who got fed up with his clothes quite quickly, or maybe they'd been donated by the family of an old country squire who had passed away. I just know that every time I went into that charity shop, I got another one of his old jackets. It kept me going for years and I'd say a good tweed jacket was always something I looked out for, still do and I've got a load of them in my wardrobe.

We often buy paintings from charity shops as well. I've got an old scene from Venice, one from Paris – to which I added King Kong fighting Godzilla for my grandson, which he loves! Lately, Kim has been adding alien ships in woodland scenes, and they look unbelievable. I'm not sure what that's called – adding your own slant to somebody else's work – but Banksy does it. He once added somebody sitting on a bench in an old painting of a lake and if it's good enough for him, it's certainly OK with us. It's amazing where you get ideas and inspiration from, isn't it?

I've got shoes, jackets, training kit – it's amazing what I have managed to find. We go to antique fairs occasionally, but they're a bit posh for us and we never buy anything because they're too stupidly expensive, but we like looking at it all, just the same.

It's a hobby of ours and we enjoy the massive flea market at Shepton Mallet where we go all the time and see the same old faces as we trawl around. Then there's the odd car boot sale, but everyone is getting too savvy, looking online to check values and what-not and we find you struggle to find many real bargains these days.

We've not done a car boot yet because it would be like that scene from Jaws, 'you gonna need a bigger van and pasting table!' Or maybe even a juggernaut because I think our style is known as maximalist – we've got things absolutely everywhere. Do we border on hoarding? Maybe – but we can still get in and out of our house, so not quite. Yet!

DOG POOP

PICKING up your dog's warm, mushy poop in a plastic bag on a cold winter's morning with the steam coming up... one of life's treats! The only question I have is, would dogs do it for us? Do they love us that much that they'd pick up our crap if they could? I don't think so. There's got to be a better way of doing it, surely? And the worst thing is, as you are about to pick it up, you've got to lick your fingers to separate the opening of the bag and as you're looking on what they've just deposited – and are often very pleased about – do you really want to be licking your fingers just before? I know I don't. It's disgusting and horrific and in this modern day when there is innovation coming out of our ears, surely there has to be a better way to collect dog shit?

I love walking my dogs, but it can be a bit of a burden sometimes because of time constraints, and mine can be little tossers, too, always running off to confront other dogs so my question is, why is everyone else's dogs nicer than mine? I say it to Kim all the time – for god's sake, look at the other dogs, then look at ours. I'm not a good dog trainer, I must admit, but I love them and that unconditional love I mentioned earlier in the book is amazing. They just want to be with you, say hello and just seeing you makes them so happy, and it just brings a lump to your throat. So, if you're dogless, shame on you!

TAKING INSPIRATION FROM OUTSIDE OF FOOTBALL

INSPIRATION is all around you all the time if you know where to look.

As I write this book, each Thursday I take Kim for her treatment. The drugs she has pumped through her are so brutal and yet Kim deals with it head on in her own way and that it is absolutely an inspiration to me.

How lucky am I to be able to go to the gym with my son and then go off to work after that when every Thursday all those people are having to go to that hospital and undergo all sorts of treatment?

I don't have to take one tablet and if I get to keep my marbles, I'll be fine, so that's what inspires me – people and how they deal with whatever life throws at them.

I try to watch very little news on TV these days because there's nothing you can take from watching bad news, which 99.9% of it always seems to be, on a loop. Where's the good news? I'd love to start my own good news channel. 'Today, Jimmy gave his sweets away to his sister because she was crying. Well done, Jimmy.' That would make me feel a bit better. Or maybe, 'Today, somebody let me out of a turning. I don't know who they were, but they were in a white Ford Focus, and I thank them immensely from the bottom of my heart.'

Wouldn't it be great to have that? So watch this space. Ian Holloway's Good News Channel... coming soon!

TEXTING 'YOU'RE SACKED'

WE'VE all heard stories about managers being sacked by owners or chairmen by a text message. Thankfully, it doesn't seem to happen that often, but it exists, and it definitely happens outside football on a seemingly regular basis.

It's disgusting and anyone who does that is a total coward in my opinion. If you have something as important as terminating somebody's livelihood, you need to be big enough to tell them to their face, rather than hide behind a text message.

You never get any real feeling or compassion with a text – our three daughters are all deaf and their texts are always abrupt because they don't have those skills we learn when listening to how things sound. Texting can be a very aggressive, cold form of communication.

I always prefer to tell people to their face if there is something unpleasant I have to tell them, whether that is letting a player go or even having to sack somebody for whatever reason, because you owe that to them to be straight and honest.

No, for me, anyone who uses a text message to convey bad

news is a coward. It's totally wrong and I'd be furious if it happened to me.

I'd rather have a carrier pigeon deliver me bad news because at least I could give it some stick and take my anger out on it before it flew back to wherever it came from – maybe tape its beak together or something. And I could always stick a note in its satchel telling whoever sent it to feck off!

ROOM 101

I'VE watched this show many times over the years on the BBC and always wondered what I'd put in there if I had the chance. Anne Robinson used to present it and then Frank Skinner took over. For anyone who hasn't seen it, the premise is that three guests get the opportunity to put three things into Room 101, which is a torture chamber, I believe, in George Orwell's book *1984*.

Effectively, whatever you choose to put in Room 101 will be banished from everyday life, so if I had three choices, I'd start with mobile phones. Everybody's on one all the time, kids can't wait to get hold of them and we'll end up with thumbs like crab claws and no vocal chords.

How have we become so totally reliant on these small devices? And if anyone were to lose one – my god – their world crashes down. I'd put them in Room 101 without a doubt and maybe people would start to communicate with each other again instead of staring at their phone.

And you wouldn't get 10-15 calls every day with somebody trying to sell you loft insulation or claim you could be entitled to compensation for an accident you've never had. Ha! Give me strength! Banish the lot of them!

My next recommendation for Room 101 would be – and I've

touched on this before – Artificial Intelligence. I watched *Terminator* with Arnold Schwarzenegger all those years ago and that bloody terrified me because it is our future! Skynet will absolutely take over one day and there won't be anything we can do about it. Apparently, there is already AI that is as clever as Albert Einstein, and we haven't even scratched the surface yet. How scary is that?

My final choice – and it's not VAR, referees, chairmen, traffic wardens or chippy football supporters – but old people. Now that might sound harsh, and people might say that I'll be old myself one day but let me explain.

Kim and I were at a garden centre, where they seem to congregate, and they just feck about in the way of your trolley and don't seem to know what they're doing or where they're going. I just felt like saying, 'I know you like plants, but can you get out of the feckin' way?'

Bimblers – that's what I call them – don't seem to realise that some people haven't got all day to kill and just want to get in and out as quickly as possible. So, stop bimbling around! Is that harsh? It probably is. I should try my calm driving approach and say 'trollies are my friend' – only they might be, but Bimblers ain't – so get out of my feckin' way!

Was it because it was a Monday that we had this issue? A 'let's go out for a bimble day'? They were everywhere. It was like a scene from *Dawn of the Dead* where the zombies are aimlessly walking around the mall.

As a bonus on this visit, I took our dog Teddy along and he did three shits on the way to the 'dog friendly' restaurant. The second and third were just mush and runny – it was vile, and I had to run to the toilets with napkins, fighting off Bimblers along the way. God bless them! Enough on this topic before I get Age Concern on my case!

ELEVATOR PITCH

MY first reaction to being asked about an elevator pitch was to ask what the hell it was. I never heard of it, but come on, you can't pitch a life-changing idea between floors when you're travelling in a lift. You've got to sit down, explain everything and go through the pitch properly. Is an elevator pitch even real? Imagine trying to sell an idea to Sir Alan Sugar between the third floor and the tenth? He'd probably headbutt you. And anyone taking an elevator pitch onboard in two minutes wants shooting. It's a stupid Americanism and I'm not having it.

HYPNOSIS

'LOOK into my eyes…' It's not something I've ever explored for myself or for any of my players. I've witnessed a hypnotist's act, making them bite onions that they thought were apples, but that's about it. The persuasion of the mind does fascinate me, and I believe it is possible to do that, but are you completely out of it or are you coherent and doing it because you think it's the right thing to do? Is everybody susceptible to it? I'm not sure, but there's a lot we don't understand and I'm very open to not shutting down ideas without being able to prove they aren't genuine. Has it ever been done to me? No. But do I think it is really possible to hypnotise somebody? Yeah, I do.

GAMBLING

GAMBLING is a terrible affliction and while there is nothing wrong with it in moderation, it can become an illness and a compulsion. I've never really understood why people in football can't bet on other games so long as yours is not involved. It's almost impossible to predict anything in football anyway, as I discovered as a pundit when my tip for relegation from the Championship – Huddersfield Town – got promoted to the Premier League in 2017. I got that totally wrong!

I've had players with gambling addictions and it's a debilitating thing because they can't control when or how they do it. Can you blame gambling for that? Not really – it's a human trait that sufferers need help with.

It can be devastating for the people around the person who is addicted, because unchecked, they can gamble everything away – all their money, their cars and even their homes.

It's an affliction and an illness and football needs to look at it all a bit more sympathetically rather than fining or banning everybody who they catch doing it. After all, there are dozens of shirt sponsors in the English game that are huge gambling corporations, and whenever you watch a match, we get a load of gambling adverts in between! Talk about the tail wagging the dog!

Does banning Ivan Toney and Sandro Tonali benefit them? Does it really get to the root of their illness? I'm not sure it does. It just gives them a load of extra time to kill. I get there needs to be a deterrent, but more help and ongoing treatment might be a better solution. Banning somebody from a pub doesn't solve their drink problem – they can nip to Tesco or Bargain Booze if they need to. Finding the root cause and then carefully weaning them away if possible, is surely the only solution.

Sporting Chance has been absolutely fantastic – ask Tony Adams and see how it helped him turn his life around. I had Clarke Carlise who was really struggling with many things in his life, and as a manager, we try to train our players physically, but what mental help are they getting? And with the abuse many of them get these days – racial, homophobic or even death threats to them and their families – it's getting harder and harder to deal with because it's everywhere, isn't it?

Another big area that seems to be ignored is life after football. How do players come to terms with life away from the game? Many struggle with not being in the spotlight and losing the routine of professional football while some don't plan well financially. It can be a big drop-off but many players find the adjustment difficult and I'd like to see more education and preparation in this area.

CASINOS

VISITS to casinos can be interesting and fun but need to be kept in check. At Blackpool, we rented out Splash World for the day after drawing four games in a row. So I decided to change things up a bit and instead of training, we went for a splash and swim, followed by a poker competition in the adjoining casino. It's a different world for me and I don't get anything from it. I work hard for my money, and I don't see getting something for nothing as a plus, really and I don't like chucking it down the drain, either.

I've seen casinos suck the life out of people and I haven't seen many casino owners or bookmakers who are struggling to make ends meet. I was with Keith Curle in a casino where he was having a little gamble and while I was sitting there, I watched a guy maybe lose £1,000 in about four minutes and getting more frantic with each bet he placed because he was running out of cash. I've never seen money disappear so quickly. I spoke with a guy who worked there a bit later and told me that the man came in every week and the money was the weekly profit from the shop he owned in town. Sometimes he won, but most of the time, he lost everything he came in with.

It's a dangerous pastime to say the least, and not like your little tipple on the Grand National or a quid or two at the Cheltenham Festival. Is it the adrenaline rush? Or is it the chase that excites? I haven't a clue because it has never sunk its teeth into me, thank God. I think it's something to do with a person's DNA – a weakness that leaves them susceptible to a gambling addiction.

I once got taken to Monte Carlo after I got QPR promoted. Gianni Paladini took me over to meet our Italian owners who were based there. We were in a swanky casino and I watched Gianni lose a load of one of the main consortium guy's money at poker, craps (very apt name), roulette – you name it – which he's presumably entrusted Gianni with. He was shouting at Gianni in Italian and I honestly thought he was going to kill him, there and then. Gianni had probably lost hundreds of thousands, and this guy spoke no English, but it was clear that he felt he'd tossed most of his money away, but by the end of the night, this guy had taken responsibility away from Gianni and somehow won it all back. It was mental.

Professional gamblers seem to use data to determine probability, but none of it seems controllable. I'd rather just buy a lottery ticket for £2 and take my chances there. I can't see that becoming an addiction anytime soon.

THE UNIVERSE

MY wife is a deep thinker whereas I'm more of a free roller. If she starts to discuss the universe and what it represents, my head starts to hurt. If Kim asks me things like what consciousness is, where is it, and is it us? Is the universe conscious? And I'll be like, 'For Christ sake, don't start that' because it mentally tires me – there's no end to it and no way of knowing. Infinite – what does that even really mean? That can't be right! Something that goes on forever – a bit like me, some might say – how can it be that there is something that never ever stops? Maybe we're not capable of understanding that and do we really need to if we're just the little ants on this planet?

How do mathematicians work out how long it takes you to get somewhere? How do they know and how can they be so clever? I'm not sure I'd want to be that different from everyone else. Or maybe I already am! And how do they even know all the wonderful things they claim are right? I'm sorry, but it just hurts my head. Or maybe I'm too thick to understand it all. At the end of the day, I'm just thinking, do I really need to open my curtains? I bet Einstein never felt like that.

REFEREES: ONLINE ABUSE & THREATS

I'LL be quite honest here and say that David Coote did his fellow referees a massive disservice when those videos came out of him calling Jurgen Klopp and Liverpool derogatory names.

He did them no favours and has made the other refs look an absolute shambles because a lot of people will assume they all act or think in a similar way.

When managers come out and say that certain referees have an agenda against their club, they only need point to Coote and say that there is the proof that it can happen.

Coote's had an absolute beast and whatever personal issues he's got, I hope he sorts them out, learns from his mistakes and maybe even gets a chance to correct them in years to come, but I think we saw in the next major public refereeing argument shortly after just what the Coote effect was. Michael Oliver's decision to send off Myles Lewis-Skelly at Wolves led to wild conspiracy theories from Arsenal fans and, to a certain extent, managers and players.

Oliver took a hell of a lot of abuse for sending off the young defender at Molineux and the fallout afterwards was completely over the top and, at times, bordering on ridiculous. Oliver received death threats as a result and police protection – and for what? A decision he made that might not have been correct but one I believe he thought was correct? And where was his VAR back-up to advise him? The whole episode has left a bad taste, and it might be some time, if ever, before the damage is repaired.

STAY HUMBLE!

I DOUBT Erling Haaland had any clue the reaction his 'stay humble' advice would get after Manchester City's 2-2 draw with Arsenal during the 2024/25 season. Haaland was heard saying those words to Mikel Arteta by Sky Sports' on-field camera at the end and to say it gave Arsenal the hump is an understatement.

Should Erling have said it? I'm not sure what the answer is, but what I didn't like was the way Arsenal behaved in the return match at the Emirates. Why was Myles Lewis-Skelly taking the mickey by copying Haaland's goal celebration? Until you've won something son, I'd advise you just get on with playing football because I wouldn't have been happy if I'd been his manager. And what is Gabriel doing in Haaland's face after they scored the first goal? The referee should have booked Gabriel for ungentlemanly conduct because that ain't right. Although Haaland did throw the ball at Gabriel's head in their previous encounter, which probably wasn't wise either.

That's a nasty bit of bad blood between the two clubs and when I was growing up, senior pros would never have allowed that Lewis-Skelly celebration to happen. He'd have had a strip torn off him and they wouldn't have done it again because if you do, you'd better be able to back it up and have a few winner's medals in your locker first. I think Haaland had won six trophies in two and a bit years at City when that incident happened – I think I'm right in saying Lewis-Skelly, who looks like a fantastic talent – had won nothing, so maybe he needs to show a bit more humility until he has? But then again, if you do win things, equally being humble counts.

As a professional, that kind of behaviour angers me and some of the lads who were senior pros when I was making my way would be turning in their grave – they are feckin' role models, you're being watched by millions of impressionable kids, what are you doing? Have a good physical battle, shake hands and move on but there are TV cameras everywhere and the more football becomes like a pantomime, the less I like it.

I can only think Arsenal are trying to create an anger within or siege mentality to retaliate in that way and you'd have to say they've always been a bit like that. Maybe it's an attitude that they believe will help them win something and we all remember how Martin Keown and company were when Ruud van Nistelrooy missed a penalty at Old Trafford many years back.

It's a win-at-all-costs attitude that I find ridiculous, and you won't ever see any of my teams act that way because I won't have it.

I'm not saying I never got involved with the odd exchange, shall we say. I remember when Micky Adams was kicking lumps out of one of my teammates and I ran 20 yards and then kneed him hard up the arse. It hurt him so much he turned around and punched me in the face! The linesman saw it and Adams got sent off – he was saying to the ref, 'Didn't you see what he did?' I apologised to Micky afterwards and he was okay about it, but I was just cleverer on the day.

Look at the best player in the world, Zinedine Zidane, he

completely lost his shit in the 2006 World Cup final against Italy when he headbutted Marco Materazzi in the chest for saying something derogatory against his sister. He was sent off and Italy went on to win on penalties – I can't believe he hasn't regretted that every day since, but that's life and people will try and draw you in, push your buttons and get a reaction out of you if they think they can. If you bite, they've won.

In tennis, John McEnroe would throw tantrums, argue with the umpire, the crowd and cause mayhem before going on to play even better, while the other player lost their focus. I wish I was like Bjorn Borg – like a goddamned iceberg who didn't let anything affect him. Dignity is a wonderful thing, but we see so little of it these days. Humility? Even less.

HAIR TODAY...
GONE TOMORROW

WIGS.. where do you even start? We had a Head of Football at QPR – a horrible fecker called Chris Gieler and he seemed to have a budget to do whatever he wanted. I really didn't like the man, and to top it off – literally – he had a selection of god-awful wigs that he used to wear. He had a short wig, a medium-length wig and a longer haired wig. He sometimes wore his longer one, told us he was going to have a haircut and put his shorter one on the next day and we were like, 'Are you feckin' serious?'

Each time he came into the cafeteria at the training ground, the lads would go through their repertoire of wig jokes. Alan McDonald found it the funniest of the lot.

He says, 'Bards, who have Wig-on got on Saturday?'

Bards would replay, 'Oh they're playing Hair-eford. Or Middlesborough at Hairsome Park.'

Gieler had the skin of a rhino. I straight asked him out once and said, 'Is that a wig?'

He went, 'No, no… it's a toupee.'

I told him there was no need to go through the rigmarole

of wearing a short, medium and long version because we all knew it wasn't real. I added, 'If my hair starts to go, it's all coming off because that is embarrassing. If you need to wear a toupee, wear a toupee but don't wear different lengths because it doesn't grow from one day to the next, does it?'

There was an Italian bloke we signed who wore a wig, too.

It looked like his dog had chewed it and was strapped on with a headband and Marc Bircham said, 'Fucking hell, what's the matter with his barnet?"

The next day he came in, it had sort of been woven in a bit like Antonio Conte – which is the best hair transplant, or perma-wig as I call it – I've ever seen. Transplant or not, a wig is a wig.

Imagine if one day my head was as bald as it is and the next day I come back from Turkey and my head is all swollen with tiny black pinpricks all over it. You know it's not my own hair, don't you? Everybody knows it's not my own hair, and that's my problem with it. Who am I kidding with this false hair? Though, as stated earlier, Conte's looks the absolute dog's bollocks. Is it a horse's tail he's had sewn on or what? He could run the Grand National backwards with that head of hair. It looks fantastic, but unfortunately, there are pictures of him from before where it looks like the dog's chewed his hair off.

You see a few hair weaves in football today and they don't look too bad, if I'm honest. Glenn Murray, Gianfranco Zola, Danny Ings and Wayne Rooney – fair play if they look decent and it makes them feel better, I don't have an issue with that.

Has Mo Salah had something done? Because his wingers were tucking back when he had his mad scientist's hairdo – but now it's shorter, and he doesn't seem to be receding anymore. Alan Shearer was left with about three hairs left at the front of his noggin for a while before he shaved it off and he looks much better for it.

Then there was the combover of yesteryear. Sir Bobby Charlton – god rest his soul – I mean, come on! Or Ralph Coates at Burnley – who were they kidding? Growing your hair behind one ear and then sweeping it across to the other ear isn't fooling anyone, is it?

I used to love my hair, but once I realised it was too wavy – waving goodbye in my case – it had to come off. My son said, 'Dad, your hair looks like the McDonald's 'M' from above.' I remember I was managing Bristol Rovers at the time and the camera panned down from above to the back of my head and it looked like I was wearing a fried egg. A car with a sun roof open or a solar panel on my barnet. Think about it – how many times do you see the top of your own head? And more often than not, it ain't a good thing when you do!

I say lose it with dignity.

Look at the people who are lucky enough to retain their natural hair – Brad Pitt for feck's sake – give him a baldy head with a combover and I don't think he'd look half as good.

When I was starting out at Bristol Rovers, Gordon Bennett insisted we all had a decent haircut. I used to have my hair quite long, so it was a problem for me, and when I went into management, I didn't mind what length my lads had their hair – though I would take exception to ponytails and manbuns, but even those are everywhere now.

Gareth Ainsworth was one of the few players I had problems with regarding hair as he liked it long and would wear headbands and all that shit. I told him that if his hairband ever came off in a game, I'd take him off as well. Maybe it was just jealousy on my part!

BEING A
BRISTOLIAN

I'M very proud of being a Bristolian and totally proud of our stupid West Country accent that often gets us labelled as farmers. The funny thing is, if you go into the middle of Bristol, there's not a farm to be seen.

Kim and I went into the centre of Bristol recently and there isn't a lot going on – it's not very nice, in fact. There's a lot of it that's looking absolutely ramshackle, but people haven't got much money, and times are hard, and it doesn't stop me being proud of my home city. I can't help my accent and no matter where you go, people assume you're an idiot because of that accent.

There's a guy who is on pretty much every day on the local radio station called Joe Sims – a Bristol City fan – and he's fantastic and he says his show is a 'proper Bristol breakfast'. And it is. I love it. He's got a strong Bristolian accent and when I first heard him, I thought, 'At last! Somebody has got it and understands!' Plus we don't have to have an interpreter, we know exactly what he's saying whereas others might not, but who cares?

The football rivalry in Bristol isn't what it should be at the moment because City are that much better than Rovers and have been for some time now. Too long, in fact. Their ground, team and finances are that much better than The Gas just now and everything's going their way. Rovers fans are sick and fed up with it if I'm honest. It gets to me because this part of the world should have a top flight club – I'll have to get my Swindon Town up there to represent the West Country! We've actually changed our name to Windon Town at the time of writing because my lads couldn't stop!

That said, I spoke to a manager the other day and he said he reminds his players they are in the bottom tier of English league football, every single day. The Fourth Division. Christ, I'd just won the League Two Manager of the Month award and it brought me down a peg or two! It's easy to think you're doing better than you are – Premier League, Championship, League One and League Two sound OK don't they – but no, we're really a Fourth Division side at the minute – who are we kidding? We have to sort our lives out.

MATT LE TISSIER

I USED to enjoy watching Matt Le Tissier as a panellist on Sky Sports' *Soccer Saturday* and, like everyone else, I loved watching him play football during his career with Southampton. Since leaving Sky, Matt's been pretty outspoken about a lot of things, but I can't help but like such a talented fella and I've done a few events with him and he's totally unique – just as he was as a footballer.

One or two things he's done or said might have been ill-judged, but everyone should have a platform to speak from and at the end of the day, everyone can relax and make their minds up about what is said. I will listen to anyone, can tolerate anything, and I won't force my opinions down anyone's throat unless they ask me for them, and only then will I tell them exactly what I think. That's pretty much the theme of this book.

Surely that's how we should live and so long as my opinions aren't hurting or offending somebody else, I can't see any harm. But if someone doesn't want me to express my thoughts because it doesn't match their thinking, who are they to tell me what I should think?

So, people like Matt, I've got all the time in the world for them and if they make mistakes, well so does everybody else.

All I know is Matt brought a hell of a lot of joy to a lot of people playing football and he was a very special talent. That seems to have been totally forgotten.

TEA LADIES, KIT MEN & CLUB CHARACTERS

TEA ladies in football are the salt of the earth. The unsung heroes few people outside the game ever hear about, often working for clubs for years and years. I believe Man City have a lady called Rose Woolrich who has served tea and sandwiches for the matchday photographers for more than 40 years – fantastic!

Our tea lady at Bristol Rovers was a legend – Vi Harris. She went above and beyond her duties of making pots of tea for everyone by finding us a goalkeeper who would go on to play for England! Ha! How brilliant is that?

It's an incredible story. Vi went on holiday to Cornwall and saw this lad playing for his local Sunday League side, St Blazey, and after the game, she told him, 'Oh, you're not bad! Let me get your number and I'll get you a trial at Bristol Rovers.' Imagine! This kid must have thought Rovers scouting network was everywhere!

So Vi told manager Gerry Francis about this kid, and he sort of brushed it off – until things got serious and she told him she wouldn't be making any more tea for him until he gave this lad a chance.

Gerry said, 'What do you mean?'

Vi said, 'Well I met this young goalkeeper on holiday, he's good, and I invited him to come and show what he could do but you still haven't given him a ring. So no more bloody tea until you do.'

And she meant it!

Gerry caved in, called the lad to come to Rovers for a few days on trial and we ended up signing him that same week! His name? Nigel Martyn – Rovers would sell him for £1m to Crystal Palace 18 months later – the first keeper to cost that much in English football and he went on to win 23 England caps, so never underestimate the power of the mythical Tea Lady!

That said, at Swindon Town, we have a tea bloke called Roger – 'Rodge the coffee bloke'. He does literally everything and the club is riddled with wonderful characters like that. Our two kit men – weird as hell, but amazing characters – they've got their own feckin' YouTube channel for Christ sake! More on that later...

Then there's our coach driver, Westy. He drives into trees, bashes into stuff all the time, our team coach looks like it used to take part in banger races and how he gets us to our destinations safely I do not know, but he's brilliant. Everything about Swindon Town and the people who work there is utterly brilliant. And as I say, there are people like this up and down the land. Unsung heroes who make working in football a joy, but when clubs come into money and new owners, they often get rid of these wonderful people and shame on them if they do because they are irreplaceable.

We had loads of priceless, good honest salt of the earth types at QPR, too – until the new owners came up and they threw them all out because 'it wasn't the right look for the club' – what a crock of horseshit.

We played Carlisle United in early 2025 and their ground is so old, it takes you back years, but they have a fantastic fan zone outside the ground and a load of youngsters giving us gyp as we came in, it was wonderful, fantastic fun. It wasn't so nice on the way out after we'd thumped them 5-1, but there you go.

We had a wonderful bloke at Bristol Rovers – Ray Kendal – god bless him. What a magnificent and genuinely hilarious bloke. He had a wonderful bouffant of beautiful silver hair and looked like Liberace's stunt double. He used to speak in a camp West Country accent and say things like, 'Ollie, I can do a thousand things, but I can't do a thousand and one.' Everybody loved him.

He used to double up by sorting the catering and then serving behind the bar in the boardroom and he'd say, 'Ollie, they've told me to freeze the sandwiches again and I've thrown them in the bloody bin. I'm not doing it!'

He did anything and everything. He washed the kit, would bring it to the training ground, take it away and wash it afterwards and on matchdays, he was our kit man, too. Then, in a never ending cycle, he'd go and serve drinks in the boardroom.

He'd have the occasional break from it all here and there, and he'd say, 'Right, I'm off to get a suntan – naked again! Sunny side up, that's me!' What he meant was he was off to a nudist beach somewhere warm. 'Get it all out. Don't be embarrassed about it,' he'd say with a twinkle in his eye. 'If you've not had your knackers out in the sun, there's something wrong with you!'

If one of the lads had a bad game and had been getting stick from the fans, Ray would tell them, 'Don't listen to that bloody lot! At least we're getting paid to be here – imagine having to bloody pay to watch us?'

What I loved about him was that he called a spade a spade and he'd never lie. He'd tell directors, 'Who'd you think you are, then? Got a business have you? Puts you above us lot, does it? I suppose you want a free whisky now, do you? The chairman will have to pay for that.'

He'd tell Geoff Dunford, the chairman's lad, 'You're so lucky you're your dad's son – god knows where you would have been without him. You've not got his class.'

Fantastic!

He was as loud as you like and he always noticed things, like, 'Oh, they're nice shoes aren't they?' and if the player wearing them was getting stick, he'd just say, 'Wear what you bloody like! Don't listen to that lot.'

He'd cook for us on the team coach to away games, and there was one time we were on our way to Leyton Orient, and the driver lost his way. So Ray called the police and said, 'We're lost, we need a police escort because there's fans everywhere.'

He was patched through to somebody in charge at the ground and this policeman says, 'Give me some idea of whereabouts you are.'

He replied – and I'm telling the absolute truth, 'I'm about halfway down the coach, why?'

The policeman replied, 'Not where you are for feck's sake – where your coach is in London!'

So Ray looked out the window and said, 'Well, there's a post office we're just passing and a Londis next to that.'

We were all cracking up because he had it on loudspeaker and the policeman shouted back, 'For god's sake, you could be feckin' anywhere! Give the phone to the driver, you bloody idiot!'

So he gave the phone to our driver and when we got to the ground, this police officer came on the coach and said, 'Where's that numpty I was speaking to? Telling me there are pelican crossings and a post box?' and Ray piped up, 'Oi! Don't be so bloody rude mate!'

There was another occasion when Liverpool were staying in the same hotel we were, our coach broke down in the car park and Ray went to ask their driver if he'd give us a bump start! He just gave him a smirk and put two fingers up to him. We had to get changed on the bus and all had to get taxis in the end, and we could see the Liverpool players sniggering at us. It was so embarrassing.

But no matter what he said, he'd always tell everyone how much he loved Bristol Rovers and what a wonderful club it was.

'It's all about the people, Ollie,' he'd say to me. He loved it.

He was a Bristol Rovers legend more than any other player could ever have been, and he made the club what it was. 'You go and do it, Ollie – you only live once', he'd say.

I'd known Ray since I was nine and like Vi Harris, their DNA runs through the clubs they work for and that's what makes football so special for me, not all the nonsense that gets the headlines today.

MORE KIT MEN...

WHEN I played at QPR we had a kit man called Ron, and he was bloody terrifying. He'd say to me in his Cockney accent, 'You don't want your extra tracksuit, do you? You can only wear one at a time. You're from Bristol Rovers aren't you – you won't be used to two tracksuits. You can have one.'

I told him if everyone else had two, I feckin' wanted two as well.

I had to stand up for myself but there were all kinds of nonsense going on between him and 'Wiggy' – Chris Gieler. They almost used to have physical fights, it was horrible to see and like a soap opera. 'Got another of your pay day players, have you?' Ron would ask Gieler. 'Twenty grand for one feckin' game? You twisted bastard. What feckin' shirt number is he having then?'

I found out Ron had his own market stall that he worked on a Sunday, and he knew everything about everybody at QPR and everything about the club. He was an absolute legend and was there for years, but oh my god, he had a tongue as sharp as a pair of scissors.

'Look at you? Want another pair of socks do you? You ain't that good a player to have two pairs of socks!' Then he'd hand an extra pair to another player and go back to the other and say, 'That's how good you need to be to have two pairs of socks, pal. How dare you ask me to pick your kit up!'

His son helped him, and he'd say things to him in front of all the lads like, 'Craig, what have I feckin' told you? What have I told you when you come into work? Shut your feckin' mouth and eat your burger! There's a good lad.'

Back in the modern day, our kit men – Jonah and Steve – at Swindon are hilarious. There is about a 12-year age gap between them, with Jonah the junior.

Like I mentioned earlier, they have their own YouTube channel called *The Life of a Kit Man*, so they were in the changing rooms one day and I said, 'What's your channel called?' One of them told me. I said, 'Shouldn't that be 'The Lives of Kit Men?' There's two of you, not one! You've named your channel wrong, you pair of feckin' muppets. You've got the life of a kit man as if there are only one of you – there's two! One of you needs to feck off! You haven't even thought about this have you?'

They have arguments that last for days where they don't talk to each other.

A few days back, Jonah rang up Steve and it went something like this:

Jonah, 'You alright?'

Steve, 'Yeah, why what's the matter?'

Jonah, 'Nothing. You just haven't rung me.'

Steve, 'What do I need to ring you about?'

Jonah, 'Nothing, it's just been a few hours, and you haven't spoken to me.'

Steve, 'What do I need to talk to you about? I'm at home with my family and we've done everything for tomorrow.'

Jonah, 'No, it's alright then. I just thought you might ring me when you got home.'

Steve, 'About what?'

Jonah, 'Nothing.'

Steve, 'Are you telling me you ring me about nothing because we've got nothing on our minds because we've already done it? What am I going to ring you about?'

Jonah, 'Oh, nothing. Forget it.'

The next day, Steve said, 'I can't forget why you rang me and asked me if I was alright. Why am I not alright?'

And it went on and on.

Steve told me and I said I didn't get it either. He said, 'Can you ask him why he called me to see if I was alright?'

So I did. I said, 'Jonah, why did you call him last night?'

He said, 'Well, we hadn't spoken.'

I said, 'You work together all day, and you hadn't spoken?'

Jonah said, 'No, we spoke. But he normally rings me.'

Steve pipes up, 'Yeah, but I only ring you if we've forgotten something. If I call you after work, normally because we have forgotten something, but we hadn't forgotten anything, so I didn't need to normally ring you.'

Jonah, 'I just thought you wanted to speak to me because you were my mate, not because you have to.'

Steve, 'You feckin' idiot. Every time I've rung you, think about what I've said when I've rung you.'

A moment passed and it was as if a lightbulb had gone on. Jonah said, 'Oh yeah, you always ask me about that or this.'

Steve, 'Yeah – so am I ringing you because I'm your mate, or because we've forgotten something?'

Jonah, 'No, it's alright – I get it. I was expecting a call from you, but it's alright.'

If they were the guys in *Dumb and Dumber*, Jonah would be the one who says, 'I wonder if my tongue would stick to that?' and gets his tongue stuck to the ice. I love them. Seek them out because they'll be stars one day.

TOILET TRIPS

THROUGHOUT my career, I've tended to get horrendously nervous before or sometimes during a game. I can't help it. I don't know if it's my age or what, but I keep nipping off to the toilet at certain moments in games. During one game at Swindon, we were awarded a penalty, and I had to go to the loo because the older I get, the more I need to drink during games. I'm going to need some kind of Portaloo on the bench so I can either have a pee – or maybe the camera might pan to me having a crap during the game. I'm lucky at Swindon because I just need to scarper down the tunnel and there's a toilet just to the first left, but most grounds don't cater for weak bladders – or worse – so it's been tough at times.

The more nervous the manager is, the more he will drink so you watch how many bottles of water they get through during a game. I watched Mikel Arteta drink about five bottles the other day and it made me think, 'Christ, he's nervous' – but it's a crazy situation because it can all go right, or it can all go wrong so quickly in this business. Everybody's body reacts differently to nerves. When I first went to Swindon – oh, my god – you could have cut the tension with a knife and it made me wonder how many people's bowel and bladder movements change just because of a football match?

I wonder if I could invent a bench with a toilet underneath so you could go during the game. Imagine a toilet roll holder fixed to the inside of the dugout? 'The Ian Holloway Portaloo Bench – let your bowel movements match the flow of the game' – I could make millions!

RECURRING NIGHTMARES

LIKE everyone else, I have nightmares. One recurring one was when I was QPR boss and I was dropping my kids off at school in Bristol every morning before I had a 250-mile round trip to take training in London, then drive back to pick them up after they finished. In my nightmare, I was always driving at full pelt when I saw the car in front stop dead, and I was steaming towards its brake lights, pushing the brakes as hard as I could without slowing down but luckily, I always woke up before impact. That was a regular dream I was having at the time.

I looked up the meaning and it said, 'You might have a car accident dream as a warning to slow down before disaster strikes, or as a sign that you're pushing yourself to the breaking point or burnout. If you want to have the best outcome, you will need to rethink, or replan, your course of action.'

And there's a lot of truth in that because I was pushing myself too hard and I was probably close to burnout given all the trials and tribulations I was dealing with at QPR at the time. I balanced it up by knowing my kids needed to go to that particular school for the deaf because the previous one they'd attended in Reading wasn't right for them. You do these things for your kids, don't you?

I've had other anxieties that have manifested themselves in dreams, then I've woken up and forgotten everything. So I started keeping a pad by the side of my bed and when the nightmare or dream had finished, I wrote down my immediate thoughts – because I would have forgotten them by morning – and then went straight back to sleep. That way, I had a record of what I had been worrying about and in the morning, I could look at my pad and figure out what the problem was.

I had so many thoughts floating through my mind, and I didn't want that to keep me awake, so writing notes worked really well for me. It was sort of cathartic in many ways because I'd read what I'd written and could see what was bothering me so much and either face it head-on or figure out a way of sorting the issue out. I highly recommend a pencil and notepad on your bedside table because you'd be amazed how your sub-conscious mind works and how many ideas you get but often can't remember in the morning.

I even picked a team based on a dream. Before I went to sleep, I'd scribbled about five or six different permutations for my starting XI for the game the next day, fell asleep and woke in the night, wrote down another team and dropped off again. In the morning, I checked my notepad and thought, 'Jesus Christ, that's a good team.'

I'd changed formation as well, so I decided to try it out and we won the game.

I've done that at Blackpool and QPR and it is amazing, the power of the mind and the way it sifts through stuff and how it manifests them in lucid dreams and sometimes nightmares. It allows you to take control of the situation, empowers you in some ways and allows you to take ownership.

Shine the light on the fear, learn how to deal with whatever it is that is worrying you and decide the best course of action. By facing your challenges, you develop your own coping strategy, and I've found I worry a lot less than I did because of the ways I've discovered I can deal with things. It's actually changed my life.

Now I'm back in football, I know the difference between real worry and issues that will solve themselves, like are we going to win? Are we going to lose? Are we going to draw? – because we'll do one of them! But I know I have to keep going and I know I've got to do my job to enable me to either win, draw or lose and anything is possible.

So, if you are going to work every day, you have to deal with whatever comes your way. Whatever life gives you, you have to learn to cope with it and sometimes that means developing a strategy because you are fearful. But most of the time, when you analyse what you are afraid of and why, you can deal with it.

Some people worry so much about what happened yesterday, or are fearful of what is going to happen tomorrow, that they are not actually living in the moment. John Lennon once wrote, 'Life is what happens to you while you're busy making other plans'

How many of us actually live in the moment? We're always worrying about what happened the day before or what's coming up tomorrow rather than dealing with the here and now and as time has gone on, I've learned to try and live in the now... in the moment I actually exist in.

Being a coach and trying to help people, I try to look at all other aspects of life and I'm a little bit jealous of people like the Dalai Lama because how much does he get right? I'd love to be that way. I'm much better at these sort of things than I used to be. Everyday life is the reality of where you actually are and maybe we all need to just say, 'Am I alright? Yes. I'm warm and I'm above ground. What a great start to the day.' I'm so thankful and appreciative of that because that gives me a chance to affect today. And I can't wait to see what is coming next.

BIG FEET

BEING in football most of my life means I've seen some strange things and one of them is feet. No two pairs are the same, some don't look the nicest and some are feckin' massive. I have one lad at Swindon with me at the time of writing – our Irish centre-half, Ryan Delaney – and I noticed his huge plates when we were in the hotel ahead of our away game at Carlisle United.

He had shorts on when we sat down to eat and Ryan is a big lad – standing at six feet, five inches – and towers over me as you might imagine. I saw his legs up close for the first time and they were massive tree trucks, and at the end of them were the biggest pair of trainers I've seen in my life. They were Adidas Gazelles and as I stared at them, I saw a potential motorhome. Kim and I had been watching this programme about people who had made motorhomes out of unusual things, and I looked at Ryan and said, 'Jesus Christ. I could make a motorhome out of those trainers if I stuck four wheels on them.'

I asked how big they were and he told me they were size 12. I asked if he wore a thin sock with them because they were massive, and the other lads started laughing. I told him that if he had my size six feet, he'd topple over. I've never seen feet like them, but they are in proportion to his body I suppose. If I had his feet and I lay down on my back with my toes pointing up, I'd be taller in height than I am standing normally.

It got me thinking and I got it up on my phone to see who had the biggest feet in the world, but in actual fact, Ryan's are positively small compared with a guy I found in the Guinness Book of Records. Apparently, there's a lad in Venezuela called Jeison Orlando Rodriguez Hernández who needs to wear a European size-69 shoe! My god! That's three campervans and a trailer.

Peter Crouch was a great bloke who also had a massive pair of feet. I had him at QPR and he was skinny as a rake back then – two snooker cues in width – and was a lovely lad who saved the club, because of the money we got for him.

I remember we'd been offered a good amount for him by one club with no sell-on clause, so I said that was no good to our chairman and that we needed a 20% sell-on. He wanted to go ahead without that, but I dug my heels in. We eventually got the sell-on written into the deal with Portsmouth who paid £1.5m for him. He was only there one season before he went to Aston Villa, and we got another £600,000 as a result of that 20% which actually saved QPR from bankruptcy.

Crouchy was a quiet lad at QPR who had to deal with a lot when he was younger because he was so painfully thin and used to get called all kinds of names and laughed at by opposition fans, but he had the last laugh – look at the career he went on to have. Spurs, Liverpool, Villa and England to name just a few and had a fantastic period with Stoke City.

Twenty years at the top ain't bad is it, and he's gone on to have a fantastic career in the media with best-selling books. Everybody loves him – it couldn't happen to a lovelier lad.

And, apart from giving us all the robot dance, he still came out with the best answer ever to a question that was put to him.

He was once asked, 'What would you have been if you weren't
a footballer?' His answer was, 'A virgin!'

TICKET PRICES IN FOOTBALL

I READ recently that Man United were charging £66 as their cheapest tickets at Old Trafford – with no concessions for kids or OAPs – that can't be right, can it? How is that value for money for anyone? That used to be the price of three football kits, but how can that possibly be value for money? If United are prepared to charge kids that much to watch a game, the owners must be a bunch of soulless millionaires who think they can do anything they goddamned want. It's disgusting and I'm told it's caused uproar with the United fans and rightly so. Liverpool's owners have caused similar concerns and god help us if we do. It smacks of Americanism. They want everything to be a brand these days, but my advice would be, don't meddle with our game. We don't want to be Americanised or become like the US – that's the scariest country in the world. God help us if we end up like some of those nuggets.

There's nothing wrong with football in this country and, in most cases, clubs remain at the heart of the local community. When teams start to do well and become successful, they seem to attract all kinds of cling-ons, and hangers-on and it all seems to go tits up. I can't stand it and maybe we need to take a leaf out of German football where you can stand in the ground, enjoy a beer on the terraces and pay maybe a tenner for a kid and £30 for an adult. That said, we have too many numpties who misbehave and can't be trusted – that's our problem and one we've had for so long. It's a fact that a lot of football fans in England behave badly and like hooligans when they've had too much to drink, and it has to be manageable.

Watch that England documentary for the Euro 2020 final against Italy – Christ that was scary. It was an alcohol-fuelled free-for-all that ended with hundreds of drunken yobs storming the barriers and forcing their way into Wembley, hurting anyone who got in their way. And you've got a guy dancing on a bus shelter thinking he's the best thing since sliced bread – why interview him and make out that it was just a bit of fun that got out of hand? The police knew what was coming, but they couldn't do anything to stop it and all because of alcohol – maybe 90% of those involved became a snarling pack of animals, and they would not have done that if they'd been sober.

So, getting back on topic, if United are laying staff off and charging their fans ridiculous amounts of money to watch the team play, they will lose that connection with their fans. It's awful, I hate it and it's not what football is about in this country, and they should be ashamed of themselves and the more it becomes like a business rather than sport, the more I hate it.

MANAGER PAY-OFFS

ONE of the things about football management that really pisses me off is how some lazy journalists assume or second-guess what a manager is paid when they are sacked or leave by mutual consent – the latter meaning they basically have had enough of you, and you've got to go and negotiate your pay-off before you go your separate ways.

I've seen it written that Jose Mourinho has been paid in full for five, six or more years of the contract he had remaining when he's been sacked by a club. That isn't true! It is true that if a club really wants you, you have the power to make sure there are certain assurances and clauses so if things don't go well, you can effectively be bought out – but I'm fairly certain even Jose would only be able to demand so much.

If you get a job from a weaker position – say if the club employing you hasn't managed to get their first, second or even third choice manager, your contract will likely be weighted heavily in their favour and your potential pay-off might be absolutely piss-poor. The thing is, you're not allowed to discuss those payments due to non-disclosure agreements, so how journalists pluck some of these figures out of the air is beyond me.

I read one story that claimed Graham Potter was given a £13million pay-off when Chelsea sacked him, but it's hard to imagine that is accurate. Someone will have looked at his yearly salary and then multiplied it by the years he had left, but I'm almost certain the severance he actually received would have been nowhere near that figure because I just don't think that happens – but people see things in a newspaper and think that it must be true. In my experience, the severance will always be between three months, six months or a year and nothing more – very rarely will it be more than that. If anyone gets 18 months' pay for leaving early, they have done very well.

COMMENTATORS

I USED to love David Coleman growing up – he was an absolute broadcasting legend and the amount of times he got things wrong or came out with unforgettable gaffes – known in the industry as 'Colemanballs' I believe, was incredible. But it just added to his aura and part of the reason he was so many people's favourite.

Some of his best, for me are:

'There goes Juantorena down the back straight, opening his legs and showing his class.'

'And the line up for the final of the women's 400 metres hurdles includes three Russians, two East Germans, a Pole, a Swede and a Frenchman.'

'And here's Moses Kiptanui – the 19-year-old Kenyan, who turned 20 a few weeks ago.'

I loved David Coleman and miss his commentary balls-ups, but I have the greatest respect for any commentator because it's a skill and an art – and one I've taken on in my media career as a co-commentator on many occasions.

I've done phone-ins, after-match radio shows, live games and god knows what else and it isn't easy when you are live and working without a script. I've been lucky enough to see football from all angles, but trying to be authentically you and saying what you really feel while staying within the bounds of what is acceptable, is difficult.

When it comes to punditry, I've always enjoyed listening to Roy Keane and Ian Wright, but I think my favourite would have to be Graeme Souness. I always felt that Souey was speaking from a place of authority having been in a Liverpool team that won everything – and he was hard as nails as a player – before then going on to manage Liverpool, Newcastle and Rangers then going abroad with Galatasaray where he witnessed the hate and passion of Turkish football in equal measure.

I just feel he's seen and lived a life – been there and done it – and particularly in his later years after his heart trouble, everything he said made perfect sense to me. I don't know if Souey has stepped away from being a pundit or just retired, but I miss his wisdom and authority. Plus he did that wonderful scene in *Boys From the Blackstuff* with Yosser Hughes when Yosser, played by Bernard Hill, says to him, 'You look like me.'

Souey replies, 'Is that right?'

Then, if memory serves, Yosser says, 'I could have been a footballer, but I had a paper round.'

Wonderful.

And I miss the old-style *Soccer AM* and *Fantasy Football League* as well with Baddiel and Skinner. We need that piss-taking because everything has become boring and too one-dimensional. I went on *Soccer AM* many times and on one occasion the band Hard-Fi were guests as well, plus there were fans from all different clubs and the banter was fantastic. Where's all that gone? Or am I missing something? I loved all of it, plus the impressions of players and managers they used to do.

While I'm on about impressions, *Spitting Image* was probably my favourite TV show and it's a shame that has gone away, too.

I think football is disappearing up its own arse and it isn't right. Bring back the fun, the mickey-taking and the banter – so long as it doesn't do anyone any harm, what's the problem?

BADLY MISQUOTED?

YOU always have to be careful what you say in football because chances are, somebody is waiting out there to twist your words or use them in a different way that you intended. You obviously learn that over time, and sometimes you have to learn the hard way,

Shortly after I took over at Swindon, I made a comment that was reported in some quarters as 'Ian Holloway blames losing run on a ghost' – I didn't say that! What I said was that I might have to try and change the aura around the club because people were getting scared that there might be a ghost at the training ground. I added I might have to ask my wife to come along and use some sage to free the spirits, but at no time did I say that was the reason we were losing games! Because of a ghost? Ha! Are you feckin' serious? That's probably the one that's been the worst misquote or mischievous misinterpretation and it's also the most recent.

I've been asked not to say anything about that anymore because the people who own the training ground said they were getting calls from other teams or organisations that hire it asking for a discount on the grounds that it was haunted! What the feck is wrong with people? That said, I suppose if you can negotiate a 25% discount, you'll try anything – even the ghost card! Life can be amazingly stupid, but whatever comes your way, you just have to deal with it as best you can.

I've nothing to worry about, apparently. My wife tells me I'm doing OK and handling things well in 'my little football career!' – ha! Let's move on.

BEST DECISION IN FOOTBALL

GOING to Blackpool and not taking the advice of my agent, I believe was the best of my football career. I'd been offered the job at Bloomfield Road, and my agent at the time said that I would become 'Bobby Driftwood' if I went there and failed. His opinion was based purely on the fact that Blackpool chairman Karl Oyston had told him he wasn't going to get paid any commission if I took the job. So, with no financial gain to be had, he advised me not to take the post because he said he believed they had no chance of doing well and I'd be cast on the scrapheap. In many ways, what he said made sense because on paper, it looked like a battle that couldn't be won with a chairman who had a reputation for being incredibly difficult to deal with.

At the end of the day, life is about feelings and how you act on them. If it feels right, follow your gut. So long as you are educated in what you are doing and understand the risks, then just go for it. Don't stop until you've achieved what you wanted to do. Otherwise you'll look back in years to come and have regrets and not like yourself because of it – and what a terrible thing that would be.

Being happy in your own skin, physically and mentally, is the key to contentment I believe. I used to look in the mirror when I was younger and think, 'Oh, I wish I had that person's hair' or 'I wish I looked like such a person' and eventually I saw the futility in all that and thought, 'What's the point of caring and worrying so much about things you can't change or don't really matter?' I learned to not give a monkey's anymore.

So, taking the Blackpool job is my best decision in football and I wouldn't change a single thing about my time there.

WORST DECISION IN FOOTBALL

IF Blackpool was my best decision, I'm going to stay beside the seaside for my worst, which was leaving Plymouth Argyle. I've said this before, but looking back, we were going so well, the players were in a good place, the fans were happy, and I shouldn't have left. End of story.

The reason I left was I wanted to give a better contract to one of my players who was playing out of his skin – David Norris – who we'd turned down £1.5million for from Stoke City. I wanted to tie him down on a new deal that rewarded him for his performances and the board wouldn't sanction it, so I lost the plot. Maybe it was because I'd already told David that I'd get him a better deal, because I believed the board would follow what I was doing, but they wouldn't back me – they said 'no'. They turned down the money from Stoke, but they wouldn't give him an improved contract and I just felt my position had become untenable. I was also dealing with Kim's mum struggling with cancer and I just got angry, didn't deal with it very well and ended up going to Leicester City who had made an approach for me.

I think about that decision and how things very quickly came to a head all the time and how those players must have felt when I walked out. A few months later, Argyle came to Leicester and beat us 1-0 and I ended up being relegated at the end of the season. I think about the Green Army and what we might have achieved together, but it is what it is and you have to deal with these things.

The next minute in life is not guaranteed and as long as you can learn from the mistakes you've made, I think you're in a good place in the world. You can't turn back the clock and sometimes you have to give things a try because I think you'll have bigger regrets if you didn't even try. Acting on what your heart is telling you rather than being scared of trying things is something I encourage people to do. Then you can never be unhappy with yourself whether you succeed or fail – at least you tried.

But hindsight is a wonderful thing, isn't it?

BEST FAN
REACTIONS

FOR me, it's not necessarily the reactions of the fans of the club I'm with that mean the most – even though that obviously means a hell of a lot – it is the reaction of the opposition supporters that can be so special.

To have opposing fans clap your team off because you've played so well, really is something else and is also quite rare. I've had it with my Blackpool team away to Nottingham Forest, where the majority of the City Ground stayed and applauded us off after we'd beaten them.

At QPR, we beat Liverpool 3-1 at Anfield in 1991 and the whole ground clapped us off. I heard a guy shout to Les Ferdinand, 'You're some player, mate!' It was brilliant and you don't get that very often – and the next generation of Liverpool fans did the same thing when my Blackpool team won 2-1 at Anfield in 2010, which says a lot about Liverpool supporters, doesn't it?

In that particular game, our fans were singing, 'Can we play you every week!?' Ha! Isn't that amazing? The Liverpool fans' reaction is certainly something I will never forget, and I am hugely appreciative of because that is a knowledgeable set of fans showing respect despite their own disappointment. As I say, it rarely happens in football so to have experienced it three times makes me very proud.

WORST FAN REACTIONS

IF I'm honest, I tend to ignore the negative fan reactions. It is what it is and it's a form of bullying because when you're in a crowd, you can shout what you like, and it can make some big-mouth coward very brave – that's how I like to see it. 'Oh, you're alright in your little pack, are you?' But it can be quite funny and part of football as well. The Tottenham fans were singing, 'Will you score a goal for us?' away to Liverpool recently when they were 4-0 down and I heard the fans of defending Premier League champions Man City singing, 'We are staying up!' during their poor run of form in 2024/25. I've heard other fans singing, 'We're winning away, we're winning away. How shit must you be? We're winning away.'

It's embarrassing if it's your club these songs are sung about, and I don't think I'll ever feel as bad in management against as I did as Swindon Town boss when we were bottom of the fourth division – because that's what it is – and 4-0 down away to Colchester United 30 minutes into the game. But football is like that and it's a great leveller. You have rise above whatever the worries or fears are and try your best and that for me is what sums life up. Feel the fear and do it anyway – there's a book out there called exactly that by Susan Jeffers and it's brilliant. Buy it and see what you think.

PUNDITS

THERE seems to be a constant conveyor belt of new pundits appearing on an almost weekly basis on TV, some better than others and some pretty average ones.

Not everyone can do it and I do miss some of the older pundits' incisive input. I loved to hear the thoughts of Graeme Souness and the old Sky Sports *Soccer Saturday* studio guests with Jeff Stelling and the guys he used to have on a few years back. It was an absolute joy.

Ian Wright is another former player I love to listen to, and Roy Keane always has something interesting to say and isn't afraid to say what he thinks, but again, that comes with the passage of time. They've been there and done it at the very top.

I try and watch now, but it's just not as enjoyable. I know things have to change and sometimes they do for the better, but I'm not sure that's the case with some of the newer pundits because good, solid football knowledge takes years and years to build up and the more you have, the more I believe younger people should take note – and that applies to life in general. Wisdom comes with age.

Remember the great Des Lynam? I'd take Des every day over Gary Lineker, because he was a trained presenter and bloody good at what he did – he didn't get a job presenting because he'd scored a load of goals in his career. It's just not the same.

There are some fantastic women presenters around. I've worked with Kelly Coates and Laura Woods many times and they are fantastic presenters – absolutely brilliant – and they deservedly front men's football, women's or any sport you care to name on a regular basis. Gabby Logan, too, is one of the best in the business and I'd watch and listen to her present all day long. These people are trained presenters and they are bloody good at what they do.

If I was invited to be a pundit on a women's game, I'd have to say, I think there are former women players who would be able to do it better than me, if I'm honest!

WOMEN'S FOOTBALL

AS the proud father of three daughters and the equally proud grandfather of granddaughters, I believe the game belongs to everybody and the fact my granddaughters can easily find a girls football club and regularly play, is amazing – that's how far we've come in a short space of time because that wasn't the case 10 years ago and 20 years ago, it would have been a near impossibility. Everyone deserves to play this wonderful game.

Seeing the Emirates Stadium full to the brim to watch a Women's Super League match, or seeing the Lionesses play in front of 80,000 fans at Wembley is utterly brilliant.

The success of women's football in this country and around the world is fantastic and I couldn't be happier with what's happening. Football is a wonderful game that can be brutal both physically and emotionally, but also hugely rewarding and if you can be part of a team it can make you a better person in my opinion. There are few other areas of life that teach you to be humble, appreciate your teammates and care about their well-being. Where else can you learn those wonderful human attributes and feel part of something special, whether you're at the top or the bottom in terms of ability? There aren't many sports where you can be totally dominated from start to finish and still end up winning, are there?

Swindon Town have a ladies team and at the time of writing, I haven't had chance to really get to know the girls or their coaching staff at the time of writing because my team is bottom of the league and we're fighting for our lives, following a typically non-top January transfer window, but I will when I have the chance. The girls have come along to some of our fan engagement events and I'm delighted by the progress women's football has made and I hope they get the parity they deserve and get to play in these wonderful stadiums we have in this country – with the crowds to match.

Our granddaughter Remi is five and she has just started playing in a team my nephew runs, and she is well chuffed with her kit – but not happy about the shinpads! And if she is happy doing what she does, I couldn't be happier. Whatever she wants is what matters, and I'm not willing her to go on and play for the Lionesses, but if she did, oh, my god! How proud would I be? But I'll get equal pleasure and be equally proud if she enjoys playing for her local club and experiencing the camaraderie this wonderful game can produce.

REFEREE STATEMENTS & TV SHOWS

WE are living in a world where cameras are everywhere, and everyone can have a platform to get their views and opinions across. Kim loves the fact that anyone with a mobile phone can share stuff, have their own YouTube channel and get their voice heard and maybe get millions of viewers – and then get paid for it!

We don't have to be spoon-fed what we watch by the five terrestrial channels anymore. If you like camping, you can find any number of people making camping videos with wonderful tips and hints, or maybe it's cookery and a million and one recipes and how to create them. There just needs to be governance of some kind and accountability to what is being streamed so nobody is getting hurt by it or being trolled.

Where was I?

Yeah, so I don't have a problem if Howard Webb wants to explain the weekend decisions in a TV show on Sky. For me, it's always been about clear lines of communication and at the end of the day, referees are human beings and occasionally they get things wrong.

I once got a letter from referee's organisation PGMOL after my Blackpool had been relegated from the Premier League, saying mistakes by officials cost my team nine points. Nine points! If we'd have those nine points, we would have finished on 48 points and equal ninth with Aston Villa. That's nine places higher than the position we finished in and probably about £5m lost in prize money, not to mention the untold riches of remaining in the Premier League. So the decisions that cost us our top-flight status, cost us a hell of lot more than just points, and changed the whole trajectory of Blackpool's future.

The explanation – in so many words – was along the lines of the officials in charge didn't think tiny Blackpool were good enough to get the big decisions against the likes of Liverpool, Man Utd and Arsenal thinking along the lines of 'Oh, that must have been a foul on Rio Ferdinand because it's a Blackpool player' that made it. Not those exact words and not necessarily those clubs – or Rio – I'm just using that as an illustration, but PGMOL asked if they could use the specific mistakes they'd highlighted to help train their members to be better and I said of course they could.

At the end of the day, it's still happening. I watched an FA Cup tie between Man United and Leicester at Old Trafford in February 2025 and Harry Maguire scored an added time winner that was clearly offside. With no VAR and no assistant referee's flag, the goal stood, and United won 2-1. I'm not saying the officials set out to make those calls, it just seems to happen that bigger clubs, in their own stadiums with a big crowd seem to get the benefit of any doubt. It's just human nature and I don't think they mean to do it, but we all have to be held accountable – I know us managers do – so how about everybody else?

Today, I try not to moan about things and just get on with it because if you do start to moan and whinge all the time, I don't think it's a good look and can come across as though you are deflecting a result or why your team is struggling. Refs are trying to be open and honest and get to grips with the technology we have, but we are still in the embryonic stage, I believe.

So allowing refs to explain on national TV and occasionally admit they got it wrong, it's got to be better than a wall of silence, hasn't it? We're never all going to agree about one single decision – everyone will have an opinion – but I say give them a chance to put their thoughts across about the decisions they made and why they made them. For me, it's a good thing and the sooner we can all hear the referee and VAR conversations during the game and follow in the footsteps of rugby union, the better for everyone.

We need to redress the balance and, like rugby, put the on-field referee back in charge and use VAR to check things for them when they request it, not the other way around.

And I believe the refs need to use the fourth official better and dominate them on the day – 'did you see that?' – 'what's your opinion on this?' and maybe even get them over to the pitchside monitor for a second opinion because there is another experienced set of eyes and ears just standing on the halfway line not doing a great deal other than getting a flea in his ear every 10 seconds from irate managers.

It took rugby a while to get used to using the technology at their disposal, so we need to be patient because we are just at the start of a long journey and there will be mistakes made along the way, but I think we are heading in the right direction. We just need to use the technology we have in a better way and let everyone in on the conversations.

SUPERSTITIONS

DO I wear an item of clothing in one game that, if we win, I wear in the next game? All the time! Superstitions or rituals are rife in football, and I admit, I'm as bad as anyone. As a player, I would put the kettle on to make a cup of coffee before the game and there would be things I had to do before it boiled because the outcome of the game depended on it – at least in my mind! You end up doing weird stuff that doesn't make any sense in the real world, but in the world of luck and superstition, if you don't follow your rituals, the end result will be bad. Ha! Even writing this down sounds like a form of madness.

But in football, it's everywhere and you see it on a regular basis, with players touching the grass before they come on, doing a hop, skip and jump as they enter the field of play as a sub.

I believe David Beckham was one of the worst for superstitions, but then again he didn't do too badly, did he? And that's the thing – the 'what if?' – what if it really does make a difference? Maybe it's like a checklist you have to tick off so in your own mind, everything is just so. It can take over your life at times.

I try not to have lucky pants, socks, Y-fronts or whatever anymore – or have a particular way of getting dressed – because it's all nonsense really, isn't it? It's all about what you do out on the pitch.

That said, there was one very special item that I carried with me in my playing days for quite a while. In May 1990, when I was at Bristol Rovers, we needed to beat Bristol City in our penultimate game of the season. If we beat them, and Blackpool in our final game, we'd win what is now the League One title. Both Rovers and City were almost guaranteed to go up, but who would be champions was yet to be decided. Mathematically, Notts County could still overtake City and Rovers and force one of us into the play-offs. As it was, we beat City 3-0 at Twerton Park and our fans were going mental.

I ended up on the balcony as we celebrated securing promotion, and I wore a hat I'd been given by the parents of a young boy who'd been killed outside his school by a car a few months before. He'd gone to run around some people who were between him and his mate on the pavement and as he stepped onto the road he was struck and killed. It was awful, but his mum and dad sent me his Rovers hat. I'd taken it with me in my kit bag ever since. I'd moved away from the club and failed elsewhere, but after 18 months back at Rovers I'd become someone's favourite player again, so that hat meant a hell of a lot to me. I thought of that kid as I celebrated and when I came to speak on the mic, I told the Rovers fans about him and felt that he was with us everywhere we went. I guess that's more sentiment than superstition, but that hat was incredibly special, and I kept it for a long time.

One of the best superstitions I ever came across was Gerry Francis at Bristol Rovers. He used to wear this big zip-up winter suit because he believed it affected our results positively. It looked ridiculous and he would wear it in the summer, and it covered everything from head to foot with double zips – one up his left leg and one up his right leg – and came right up to his cheek and when it got really hot, he'd zip it down to his shorts. And it was stinking in there, too! He did it because we were winning, and I think we ended up champions in the 1989/90 season and he wore it pretty much all the time. It used to walk to the washing machine on its own!

I've had a lot of players who wanted to wear a specific number. I used to ask them, 'Can't you play without that number on your back, then?'

Because I was the way I was, I sort of understood it and tried to give them the number they wanted, but often it meant playing in one they weren't happy with.

When squad numbers came in, it was much easier, but there was still a reluctance to wear No.12, 13 or 14 because that was associated with being a sub when we had 14-man matchday squads. Nowadays, those numbers don't mean a thing.

I've experienced players who've said that they need to do this or that and I've just gone with it, but you can very rarely change something that someone does if it means they think they're going to play well.

Then there was the voodoo curse on my goalkeeper...

Something very odd came to light after Blackpool were relegated in 2010/11. After we'd been condemned back to the Championship, our goalkeeper Richard Kingson's wife wrote a letter to the local paper to apologise because she said she'd put a voodoo curse on him! She later retracted her claim. I honestly don't know any more than that, but it's another 'what if?' moment. We went down by one point that year, so who knows? It could only happen to one of my clubs!

That said, I'm sure there was a gypsy curse on Birmingham City stretching back years, so when Barry Fry took over, he peed in a bottle and then poured some on all four corners of the pitch. Given the Blues' lack of trophies over the past 50 years, I think he might have needed a bigger bottle!

I got a car at one club, and we went on a run of games without winning so I got rid of it because I associated our poor form with driving that car – how stupid was that? As if a car can affect your team's performances, but this is what can happen with superstitions and rituals if you let them get inside your head. It can take over and I think we've all got a bit of that in us if we're honest.

How many of you reading this still salute a magpie? If I see one on its own I will still look the other way unless I see two of them. Again, madness – but millions of us do it! I think we're all a bit warped and twisted at times, I really do.

PHOBIAS

IT'S a fact of life that human beings have phobias and debilitating fears. In football, the phobia that always jumps out for me is Dennis Bergkamp's fear of flying. I think there were a number of reasons Dennis didn't like to fly – or at least reasons that have been attributed to it. One is that there was a plane crash involving Dutch youth team players that were friends of his, while another is that he decided he hated flying in small, private planes and so made the decision he didn't want to do that anymore. There is another story that mentions a Dutch journalist claiming he had a bomb at the 1994 World Cup and the plane Dennis was on was grounded as a result. Or perhaps it's bits and pieces of all those alleged incidents, but wow! How inhibiting is that for the player and for his club at the time, Arsenal?

Their best player wouldn't fly with the team and only wanted to go by rail, car or boat and, in many European games and pre-season tours, he didn't travel at all. For me, Dennis would have had to have flown if he was playing for one of my teams, no matter how brilliant he was because that was what he was paid to do and, as one of the best players in the world, his absence would have seriously affected the team's chances of winning major trophies. It also disrupts the team ethic and sort of sets you outside that bubble. OK, domestically, he was part of a wonderful Arsenal side that won many trophies, but Arsenal have never won the Champions League, and you wonder whether they might have done if Dennis had always been available when fit.

I'm not treating his fear lightly and it's actually quite a brave thing to admit when you are a hero to millions because you're revealing a weakness in your psyche. But as a top footballer, flying is part and parcel of your life and there can't be many phobias which are more damaging for a player than the fear of flying.

CARDBOARD 'CAN I HAVE YOUR SHIRT' SIGNS?'

DO I have an opinion on these? Yes! To be honest, I've thought of making my own to respond with if I see one in the crowd aimed at one of my players – I'll just stand there in front of them holding up a cardboard sign written in crayon with: 'Go and buy one from the club shop.'

Seriously, I don't get it. I know it would be great if your favourite player hands you his shirt, you maybe get it signed, framed or even sell it on eBay – but I also think it's damned cheeky and I really don't like it.

I've not seen any at Swindon yet but that could because our fans have given up asking! If the lads give a shirt away now, they've got to pay for it.

We've got nowhere near enough medium sized shirts left at the time of writing and one of our kit men was asking me if I signed any players during the 2025 January transfer window, could I make sure they were size large! I said, 'Shut up you

idiot!' I swear he was serious, too! Adidas are our kit manufac-
turer and charge us a fortune, and when I asked for a longer
coat for the winter, they only had short ones, so I ended up
wearing my own coat. I bet Mikel Arteta doesn't have to do
that.

Life in the lower leagues, eh?

BEST & WORST ADVICE

ADVICE is a wonderful thing and, if correct and delivered in the right pitch, can really impact your life positively. I've got a few examples that affected my playing career in a big way.

The first was from Gordon Bennett, who was chief executive at Bristol Rovers. I was just a kid at the time, and I remember him saying to me, 'What I like about you is you want to make it yours. So try and make it yours, each and every time you play.' I asked what he meant, and he said, 'Wherever that ball goes, ask yourself whether you can you make it yours?

'Don't doubt it, if it is in your vicinity, try and make the ball yours and try and think about how you can make that happen. If you do that, you'll always be ready.'

It sounds so simple, but as a combative midfielder like I was, it meant I was never out of the game. But as you go along, you learn the best pieces of advice are always the simplest.

My dad used to add bits and pieces of advice here and there, too. He'd tell me to never let the ball bounce if there was any way of getting to it first – get to the pitch of it and control it, so you don't have to wait for anything – or anyone – and are effectively one step ahead.

But I'd say 'make it yours' is the most helpful and sensible piece of advice I ever had and one that stuck with me more than anything else. It was one of the first things Gordon, a magnificent gentleman, ever said to me.

I tell my lads at Swindon the same thing – make the ball yours and also, 'What do you want to be? Someone who lets it happen, or somebody who makes it happen?' So that essence of competitiveness and trying to get an edge on your opponent all comes from that kind of advice and if it works for you, it sticks, and you never forget it.

At QPR, Ray Wilkins – a lovely bloke who I had the utmost respect for – was having a chat with me about retaining possession. As we walked back to the changing rooms I said, 'I don't ever want to give the ball away,' and Ray said, 'Well, I don't look at it that way. I don't ever want to be caught with the ball – if you're caught with the ball it means you don't know your next pass and you're not thinking the right way.'

What he said made perfect sense. I took that into my game immediately and it made a hell of a difference. He added, 'You have to keep hold of your self-esteem too, because your confidence belongs to you, son.'

The worst piece of advice I ever received was from Bobby Gould when he was Bristol Rovers manager. I was only a kid at the time, and I told him I was splitting up with my girlfriend – Kim – and that I was really upset about it. He just said, 'Get over to Ibiza, have a feckin' holiday and see how many girls you can meet over there. Then get a shot up your arse when you get back in case you've caught anything.' That's actually a much nicer version of what he said.

So, I was struggling mentally and emotionally, and his

solution was to meet other girls – and in a pretty horrible way as well, as far as I was concerned. Me and Bobby didn't really get on, but, considering that same girlfriend I was about to split up with is still by my side, some 40 years, four kids and eight grandkids later, I think I got that one right, not Bobby. Horrendous.

Everybody is different and I guess different advice works for different people. I've always tried to help and guide as best as I can, and if any of my players were ever struggling, I will always do everything I can to help them. Steven Caulker and Clarke Carlisle were two of my lads who really went through tough times, and it was wonderful to get messages from them later on when they felt better, but I try and say something to everybody because I want them to be better people before they are better players. They have a responsibility being a professional foot-baller and I want them to care about everyone else as well as looking after themselves properly. If you can do that, then you are starting to become part of a team environment rather than just looking out for yourself.

I guess another really bad piece of advice I received was when I was manager of Grimsby Town, having placed my trust in the wrong people.

We were playing away and I had the someone I thought I could trust doing our opposition scouting reports and he told me the opposition played a totally different way to the way they actually played.

So, I prepared my lads to play a certain way to deal with their style, instead of checking the video of their last game myself. If I had, I'd have seen they had a diamond and if you play that formation effectively, you can outnumber the opposition in the wide areas.

The opponents did play the diamond formation incredibly

235

well, and we went out there expecting something completely different, but as soon as the game started, I thought, 'Oh my god – that's a diamond' and it was obvious we were immediately being overrun because we had three up front and that won't work against that formation.

I tried to change it from the touchline, but my lads didn't understand what I was trying to convey and by 33 minutes, it was already too late because we were several goals down. We'd had no practice at playing against a diamond and were setting traps for the formation I'd been told they played, but no one was there to trap, and my lads were playing the way we'd prepared in training. I'd had an awful feeling beforehand as I sat in the empty stands (during COVID's behind-closed-door matches) that something just didn't feel right.

Had we prepared differently, would it have been a different outcome? I'm not sure, because they played the way they did so well, but when your team is not that good, you spend a lot of time trying to stop the other team from playing. I picked the wrong team and had the wrong players in the wrong positions.

I should have let that analysis guy go the moment I joined. But he'd stitched me up and I made sure he was on his way after that incident. I guess that qualifies for bad advice, but it was a pretty miserable time overall at Grimsby and I certainly made mistakes during my time there.

Football is a very selfish game at the best of times and my job is to not make players selfish, but to be part of a team that cares and looks out for one another. If I manage to do that, you usually have half a chance. But managing in a pandemic proved to be the worst experience of my career and one the people of Grimsby still haven't forgiven me for.

TRAFFIC WARDENS

TRAFFIC wardens are a bit like referees really, aren't they? They are about as popular as referees, that's for sure. Traffic wardens are a different sort of people, I think. I know they are just doing their job, but for feck's sake, do they have to look like they are enjoying it so much? They are always looking to do someone and nine times out of 10, the joy on their face when they do is just horrendous, isn't it?

I'm probably not the best person to talk about traffic wardens because I once tried to throw a Dyson vacuum on a warden's foot, which would have gotten me in a whole world of problems. I'd been held up in a shop where I was buying this Dyson and when I got back to the car, there he was with his ticket freshly posted on my windscreen. 'What the feck do you expect me to do?' I asked. 'I'm five minutes late because the guy selling me this took an age.' But he just gave me a smarmy look and I'm afraid it was like a red rag to a bull and my new box-fresh Dyson was suddenly heading in his direction. A clear case of do as I say, not as I do! I looked a right tosser in truth, and I got told off by the police afterwards, 'What are you doing, you idiot?' but never mind! I'm not proud of it, but I think it's worth sharing.

It is the glee traffic wardens have, that moment of absolute power… you just know they are loving it. I have a theory that they were the kid at school that never got included with anything and they've held a grudge ever since, so off they go, find a job where they can get a bit of payback and even the scores out a bit.

A lot of these 'Karens and Kevins' are traffic wardens – self-entitled people who enjoy shouting and bawling at good honest folk just going about their daily business. People in banks, supermarkets and delivery drivers – plus loads more – get hammered by these Karens and Kevins whose basic aim in life is to just try and piss everyone off with their self-entitlement. Look them up on YouTube – they're everywhere!

My final message to traffic wardens? I know you are doing your job and it's not a popular one but just don't look like you are enjoying it so much when you are handing a ticket out.

Let's move on…

CRICKET. WHAT'S THE POINT?

PEOPLE often ask if I like cricket or not – and here's what I tell them. Imagine the first person who came up with it, 'Lads – I've got a great idea. We're going to play a new game I just thought up called cricket. First off, we need to chop that tree down and make six sticks, then find some twigs to stick along the top of them, then stick them in the ground on some really flat grass and then put some markings down. Then we need 22 guys. Some of you will stand around on the grass, most of the other team will sit in a hut for a few days drinking tea and eating sandwiches and then two of us will strap these weird things to our legs, make some big flatter sticks, put some head protection on and then that bloke there is going to throw a red rock at us at about 90mph while his teammates all stand around watching. Oh, and both teams will wear white, and we will rub that red rock against our crotch so it ruins our trousers.'

If somebody had pitched that idea to me, he wouldn't have lasted five minutes and it would have been a case of 'feck off, mate!' I don't know who thought it up but it's the worst idea I ever heard.

Football was simpler – get a pig's bladder, blow it up and stick jumpers down for goalposts. Tennis might have started with square rackets, but the idea was good – a bat with taut wire and a ball that bounces, and all you have to do is hit over a net. At least the ball wasn't square as well, or it might never have taken off. Simple! You might have guessed I'm not a cricket fan. I actually use that 'birth of cricket' story at any cricket club after-dinner speaking I do, and they laugh their heads off – because they know I'm right! Cricket. It's just not right, is it?

I love most sports, but the ones you have to be patient at, I'm usually not that good. I do love snooker and used to have my own snooker room, once. It's a brilliant game and so skilful, but completely useless in your everyday life! It's not a cheap game, either. One of my life ambitions was to have a snooker room in my house, and when I eventually got one, it was a dream come true. But my god, it comes with some baggage! You need a reinforced floor and the table has to be built rather than delivered because of its size and weight. However, it is a truly wonderful sight in a darkened room with that light hanging over the green baize. Fantastic! But I also found when we left that house that nobody actually wants a snooker table, so I needed to give it away in the end. Me and my dad used to watch *Pot Black* on the BBC, but on a black and white TV, all the balls other than the white looked black! It should have been called 'Pot Something'.

The dedication you have to be to become a great snooker player is ridiculous, but that's what I love about sport. You have to be totally obsessed to get to the top and it's that dedication that I love.

TV QUIZ SHOWS

KIM and I love them. One of our favourites is *The Chase*, but would I like to go on it? No! The contestants always look intimidated, standing way below the Chaser on their perch at the top of the money board. It's like going to see your bank manager with the raised and lower seat scenario meaning they will always be looking down on you. I might be OK with the three choices part against the Chaser, but in the one-minute round of questions, I'm not so sure. You either know them or you don't.

Who would I like to take on the most in *The Chase*? Probably The Beast, I love his arrogance and if I could beat him, I'd be made up, but I'd probably take the lower offer of £1,000 or something just to get back. I'd never take the big offer because they don't get many wrong and if you get one wrong, you're almost out.

It's great entertainment and we love those shows. *Pointless* is another – I don't get many of those questions correct, if I'm honest, which pisses me off. It just frustrates me, and I think if I went on, I'd be fuming because I'd know some of the answers but wouldn't be able to remember them at the time – which is pretty useless.

I'd be alright at *Tipping Point* because you get three choices of answers if you get to the final. Plus it's like the 2p arcade game, which I can handle. And I'd start with my weakest topics first and if physics or cooking appeared, I'd give it up. I burn beans, eggs, toast… you name it, and physics makes my head hurt.

BEST PITCH/ WORST PITCH

FOR me, the best pitch I ever played on was at Old Trafford – that was somewhere I always wanted to play at least once in my career and when I finally got the chance, QPR beat United 4-1 in 1992, which was off the charts. Sir Alex left a few of his big hitters out, we surprised them on the day with the way we played, and Dennis Bailey hit a hat-trick.

I remember being in the toilet that day when Gerry Francis was doing his team-talk beforehand because I was that nervous. He said, 'Where's Ollie?' I shouted, 'I'm in here, I can hear you from here!' But it all turned out well in the end and though walking out on the Old Trafford pitch is something I'll never forget, I guess it wasn't the greatest pitch because it was raised with steep edges, and you felt like you could fall off and hurt yourself. It actually felt like United wanted you to fall off, which was quite intimidating, but I suppose their own players had the same issue.

My least favourite venue is Dagenham & Redbridge's Victoria Road. I hate that ground. I took my Grimsby Town side there in the pandemic during the FA Cup. The overall experience was absolutely horrendous from start to finish. We went 1-0 down, pulled it back to 1-1 and then conceded two late goals to lose 3-1. Knocked out in the first round to a non-League club and I was just sat there in an empty stadium with COVID everywhere thinking, 'What on earth am I doing here? What are any of us doing here?' That was my worst football experience without a shadow of a doubt.

The worst pitch was probably at Plainmoor, home of Torquay United, but they're a good club and at the time of writing, my old mate Neil Warnock was there in an overseeing role so hopefully we'll see them back in the Football League again one day because the more south west teams there are, the better.

I must add, pitches aside, there was one moment at an away ground I'll never forget. My Blackpool were at Craven Cottage the day they unveiled the Michael Jackson statue in 2011 – my God, what was all that about? It was goddamned awful! I was expecting some kind of bronze or marble masterpiece, but it was all garishly coloured and looked more like Bobby Ball. His face resembled Michael Myers out of the *Halloween* horror films. Jesus, what a monstrosity that was.

STOKE CITY ON A WET WEDNESDAY NIGHT

ANYONE who knows me will know that Tony Pulis is a very good and very old friend. We go way back to our apprentice days at Bristol Rovers and I've nothing but respect for what he's achieved in the game. He's probably best known for his two managerial spells with Stoke City (2002 to 2005 and 2006 to 2013). I remember taking on Stoke at the Britannia Stadium during that period and there was one occasion when a Stoke fan attacked our goalie. There was a big fight when Gerry Taggart did something to our keeper, then got sent off and Taggart was waiting for our keeper in the tunnel – it was all horrible – but it wasn't anything to do with Tony and that's not why I'm highlighting him here.

Tony created something brilliant at Stoke. The whole place was intimidating because of the way they set about you. The Stoke players were physically imposing, their style of play was tough to handle, and they were incredibly difficult to defend set-pieces against. There's nothing wrong with any of that. In fact, Arsenal try to do something similar today, with their corner routines and blocking tactics. In my opinion, Stoke were better because they set the bar.

Tony's Stoke City had a lot of different ways of getting at you. Rory Delap's throw was a hell of a weapon, and they liked to go long to a big man up front and they were almost unique in their style. A lot of clubs couldn't deal with that. They got roundly criticised for their playing style, but Christ it was effective, and I don't think anyone else could have made Stoke City away feared the way Tony did with the players and budget he had at his disposal. He played to his team's strengths and Stoke have never come anywhere near to being the team they once were since he left. If that same team were in the Premier League now, I believe they would be a top 10 side.

Like I mentioned earlier, what I don't like is Big Sam Allardyce and Tony being labelled by certain journalists or pundits in a derogatory way, as if their football hadn't moved with the times, because they couldn't be more wrong in my opinion. They were finding a way with the players they had and because Arsene Wenger thought it wasn't fair when he took his Arsenal side to the Britannia. He didn't like the tactics his team had to face because it wasn't 'purist' football – ha! Look at Arsenal now! They are called the 'new Stoke City' by some people! I bet Arsene never saw that one coming. That said, Arsene still had two six-foot two centre-backs and two six-foot four midfielders. They hardly ever beat Stoke as I recall. It's always about adapting and that's why Tony Pulis and certain other managers don't get the credit they deserve.

During the 2024/25 season, Nottingham Forest played with maybe 35% possession and look at how good they have been. They bucked the trend, played to a style their players were suited to and showed that you don't have to play 50 passes in front of your own goalkeeper to start a move off.

It's a wonderful game isn't it – full of opinions, different styles and ideas – so let's celebrate the managers that go out on a limb, do things their own way and still have success. I'm sure Arsene would agree!

TAKING JOURNALISTS TO TASK

IF somebody writes something derogatory about you or your team, the bottom line is you don't have to take it. If you don't agree with what they're saying, call them out and, if necessary, make them apologise. When I was Bristol Rovers manager, our two strikers Jamie Cureton and Jason Roberts were on fire. After we drew 0-0 with Bristol City, a journalist claimed in his match report that if City had my two strikers – who, in that game, were rubbish by the way – then City would be a team that Bristol could be proud of. Wow. The other lads were getting a bit cheesed off with us being labelled a two-man team because of the goals Jamie and Jason were scoring, and I was left spitting fire. I couldn't believe what this guy had written. We hadn't played well, but we had drawn 0-0 against our biggest rivals, and my defenders had been magnificent, but then I read something along the lines of, 'If only City had Cureton and Roberts up front...' If you're going to write huge statements like that, you'd better be able to back that up my friend!

So, I invited him to the training ground. He didn't know why, but in fairness, he had the guts to come along anyway. I knew why and for once, I was going to make someone front-up to what they'd written and experience what their reaction was like first-hand. It's all well and good opinionated football reporters tapping away on their laptop, but would you write the same crap if you actually had to say it to the players in question? I sincerely doubt it.

So, when he arrived, I went to meet him, and I was in no mood for niceties. I said, 'Right, you are going to apologise to my team, you bastard.' I took him into our meeting room where all my players were sitting down. I had the two centre halves stand up. I said to the journo, 'Right, now tell these two – who you only gave five out of 10 each – just how well you think they played, you arsehole and if you two don't agree with what is being said, make sure you let it be known.'

Then, I stood by Curo and Jason Roberts and said to the journo, 'How dare you! I'm trying to educate these two to be better players. They didn't play well, but you say they did in your match report, and you don't mention my defenders or how well they played. These two (Cureton and Roberts) were useless on the day and you're telling them they're great and by the way, when you're making a statement about my home town, be careful what you say. I'm already very proud of my team so how dare you insult my club by saying 'Bristol could have a team to be proud of. Aren't you proud of us when we're working on the budget we are and still wiping the floor with you lot over there? How can you give him eight out of ten and him five? Because that's what you did. Are you watching the same game? Are you watching the right game?'

Bear in mind this was nearly 25 years ago when I was more of a hot head. I know I shouldn't have done it and that it was bang out of order, but sometimes I think people should be held accountable for what they say or do. My lads loved it because I'd stood up for them and they were having me all day long because of the way I was with them. I just wanted to treat them the way I would want to be treated, and I knew that if I was a player who had a manager who would do that, I'd give my all for someone who believed in me like that. After my rant, I said thanks to the reporter for having the bottle to come over and he went on his way. I was a stroppy little shite with the media and got it totally wrong at the time, but it's not always wise to play and manage the club you support because sometimes you just let your emotions run wild.

ROOM SERVICE

ONE story I never get tired of retelling is the 'room service' incident I instigated while managing Blackpool. I didn't often get told off during my time as Blackpool manager but there was one occasion when I got called into Karl Oyston's office where he was holding a bunch of receipts in his hand. He asked me, 'What's going on? Have you been keeping your eye on these players?' I asked him what he meant, and he said, 'Well, we're feeding them but then they're ordering room service.'

I said, 'Nah, my lads wouldn't do that.'

'Well, who's ordering this food then? Look at these hotel bills?'

I had a look through them and there were chips and beer on an invoice charged to the club. I told him that wasn't right, but he said, 'I'm telling you, keep your eye out for it. I'm not paying for this again after we've just fed them half-an-hour before. They should bloody pay for it themselves and you should know what they're eating and drinking.'

He was right, too. And it put a bee in my bonnet because I decided to catch the culprits red-handed. I didn't say anything to the lads, but on our next away trip, I asked them at the evening meal if they were all OK, had they eaten enough and whether they needed anything else?

Nobody said anything, so when they went back to their rooms, I went to the receptionist and told her that if any of my players ordered room service, she was to come over and tell me because myself and the backroom staff always ate slightly later. I told her not to let them know, but to bring the order to me so I could deliver it personally.

I had ordered my starter, but it hadn't arrived yet when the receptionist came over and said that one of the lads had ordered some chips and two pints of lager. She said she had told them no, but I told her to call them back and say actually, it was fine. We hatched a plan that when the food and drink was ready, she was to let me know so I could go up with the member of staff and then I would hand it over.

It turned out to be the room of Brett Ormerod and Keith Southern – two of my senior players and I was thinking, 'Hang about. What's going on here? They know the rules.' So when the young lad serving the food knocked on their room, I knew they'd look through the little spyglass in the door first. So I waited until they did and then quickly took the tray as I heard the door being unlocked. I just stood there with the two pints and the bowl of chips. Brett opens the door, sees me and his jaw drops, 'Oh hello gaffer!'

I said, 'Hello Brett, now move out the way and I'll bring your room service in!'

I put it down in their room and said, 'What are you pair of nuggets doing?'

They didn't know what to say and sat there like two naughty schoolboys so I said, 'Tell me, if you were at home on a Friday evening before a match, what would you do?'

Brett said, 'Gaffer, it's OK, I always have a drink and it's fine.'

I said, 'And eat chips?'

He said, 'Yeah.'

I looked at Keith and said, 'Well, what about you?'

He said, 'No, I don't usually but for the last few away games I have because I'm with him.'

I bit my lip and then told them that it was OK, they could keep doing it and that this order was on me, but going forward, they had to pay their own bills for any room service because the chairman had found out. They both looked relieved and just laughed. The moral of the story? I'm not sure there is one, but players will do something anyway if they really want to and so long as it's in moderation and doesn't affect their game, I'm OK with that.

SUITS YOU

TRAVELLING away, playing at home or attending events – I absolutely love it when my lads look smart and part of the same team. I had to fight hard to get my players suits and club track-suits at Blackpool, so when I came up against somebody who didn't want to conform, it caused one or two problems.

I had one player who wanted to pray whenever he needed to, so I told him that would never be an issue. If he needed to pray before a game, come in his club tracksuit and then go home after the game in it.

'But if you are voted the man of the match,' I told him, 'I want you to wear the club suit.'

He said, 'No, I'm doing that.'

I said, 'Excuse me? Is it because of any particular reason?'

He said it wasn't. 'It's just not me and I'm not doing it.'

He had to go, sadly. How could I have one player not follow the club guidelines? It wasn't anything to do with religion – he just didn't want to wear a suit. I was trying to promote the feeling of camaraderie and that we were all in it together, but he wasn't having any of it. You can get away with that if it is accepted by the group, but if it isn't and it offends the others, you have to take the appropriate action.

I don't need to name the player in question, but he tried to make it as though the problem was because he prayed, and I wasn't having any of that. I said he could wear his tracksuit and just put the top half of the suit on if he won man of the match honours so he could have his picture taken in it – and then get dressed again, because I fought with the chairman to get it. But no.

I spoke to the lads to see if they had any different thoughts on it, but the general feeling was, 'Get rid of him, gaffer' or a few who were a little more blunt – 'fuck him off, gaffer'.

If you look rough, untended, and as though you don't care, I don't like it. If you're turning up for the club, I want you to look like the club would want you to look. I don't want scruffy, and I don't want somebody's arse hanging out.

If you're in a club suit or tracksuit, there is conformity, and you look like you belong to something. It's like having meerkats – you have to have them all standing and facing in the same direction, because if half of them are looking one way and half the other, you've got problems, and you'll get divisions.

Being a manager is about not creating divisions and being aware of what can be divisive and not allowing it – it is so vital to conform because we all have to believe in the greater good (as they say in the movie *Hot Fuzz*!). You can have one or two slight variants, if you like, but overall, we all have to be on the same page.

PRIDE IN YOUR HOME TOWN

AS you are no doubt aware, things didn't go well for me during my time at Grimsby, but I did care for the club and the town. If I could do my time there again and it wasn't in a pandemic, I would do a lot of things differently.

It was the only time we'd lived on the East Coast, and one day, Kim and I were walking through a shopping centre in town when I saw two youths. One of them was eating a chocolate bar and I watched as he threw half of it away over his shoulder and into a shop window.

I said, 'Oi! You! Go and pick that up! Would you do that in your nan's house? The bin's over there, so go and pick it up, or I will. It's disgusting. You've no pride in your town.'

He said, 'Well, this town's a shithole, isn't it.'

I told him, 'It doesn't matter what it is – you've just made it worse.'

He took it quite well, picked it up and put it in the bin, but word somehow got around that Ian Holloway had told this kid off, and at the time, the people of Grimsby loved it because they could see I cared about their town. I didn't want it to get out, but it did and I'm still not sure how. It was all about taking pride in your surroundings and trying to make things better, and that's the message I tried to promote at the football club while I was there. We knew it wasn't the best place on the planet, but we had to try and make things better than they were.

'YOU'RE MESSING WITH THE WRONG GUY!'

IF you've ever watched the film *Planes, Trains and Automobiles*, you'll recognise the title of this entry as a line that Steve Martin says. And there was one occasion when I was Plymouth Argyle manager that a lippy fan was definitely messing with the wrong guy at the wrong time.

We were going well in the league but after three away games in succession, I made a comment that the lads looked a bit leggy and tired in the third match. Then we played Sheffield Wednesday at Home Park and played them off the pitch for most of the game but somehow lost 2-1. Things were coming to a head, and I was becoming increasingly frustrated with the board's stance on bringing some fresh legs in so when I'd held my post-match press conference, I walked out of the ground to get my car and go home.

But there was one guy waiting for me.

'Tired again, were they?' he said as I passed him.

Red rag + bull. I steamed over to him. 'Pardon?'

'Were they tired again?'

I said, 'Look, I never make an excuse, mate. What did I say?'

'You said they were tired – they're bloody professional footballers, they should be able to run about for 90 minutes.'

'No, I didn't say they were tired. What I said was – and it's in the programme you're holding which you aren't clever enough to read my old friend – I'm asking the same players to do too much – now what does that mean to you?'

I suppose I was a bit aggressive, but he'd taken a stance I didn't like, and he was now very aware of that. He said, 'Oh, I'm not having a go at you, Ollie.'

I said that actually, he was and that he should wait outside the boardroom door and ask them why they aren't getting some more players in. I then added, 'Now did we deserve to lose today?'

'No.'

'Well, there you are then. When are you going to wake up and realise who it is you need to shout at?'

A bit of a crowd had gathered and with the mood I was in, I decided I best leave it at that. I'd said my bit and maybe a bit more!

INFLUENCERS

I'VE spoken about some of the people who influenced my career in the Best Advice entry. Gordon Bennett of Bristol Rovers was an incredible man and a lot of the stuff he said to me as a kid is still relevant to me today in my management career.

Bill Dodgin Senior and Bobby Campbell at Rovers were two senior coaches who were constantly there during our youth team training sessions every Tuesday and Thursday. When you know you have two first-team coaches joining in, for me that was massive because they were imparting the same knowledge to us that they were giving to first-team players. I'm not sure you got that at every club and a lot of that was down to the inclusive family atmosphere that Gordon Bennett had created at the club. He'd also have former players who had just retired get involved with training the kids and it was all a wonderful grounding for me and all the other lads.

Don Megson wasn't at Rovers that long as manager, but the things he said were good and he gave us sound advice that made a huge difference about the work we had to do and the way we needed to behave.

Harold Jarman was another. I'd just signed my first pro-fessional contract at Rovers, and we had some non-contract players who trained on a Monday night by Harold who was a goal-scoring right winger. I'd play at the weekend and train as normal, but I always made sure I attended Harold's Monday night sessions because he was so good as a coach. He ended up as our physio (I mentioned him earlier), but he should have been a coach because a lot of those lads like Steve White, Paul Randall, Phil Purnell, Larry Lloyd and Gary Penrice – among others – all went on to have great careers and I put it down to the legend that was Harold Jarman – and what a great bloke to boot.

Then there was Gerry Francis, the manager who believed in me so much at Rovers. He used his own money to buy me when he moved to QPR because the club couldn't afford it and he believed in me so much – imagine that? A manager spending his own hard-earned cash to buy a player? And imagine what that does for your confidence? Gerry and I have been friends for more than 40 years and there are few people in football who have influenced my career and life more than he has.

TAPPING UP

'TAPPING up' – illegal contact from other clubs to a player or manager – it goes on all the time. And thank god agents now admit it does because players being contacted by outside sources has always happened and is almost impossible to stop. Whether you're a player or manager, other clubs are allowed to speak with an agent on your behalf whether you are contracted or not and while clubs wanting the individual involved will deny that they make these illegal approaches, it's a lie because they goddamned well do!

Everyone in football knows when a player's head has been turned, either because they've been informed of another club's interest or by reading it in the media with renowned sources. Their agent will be contacted by a club interested and be told that they want their client, the agent in turn will inform the player they represent and it can lead to them completely losing focus at the club who are paying their wages – and anyone who thinks that doesn't happen is living in cloud cuckoo land.

The messages that will be exchanged will be along the lines of, 'Oh, we really want you to join us… we might get you before the end of the year… how much do you want? We'll double that…' and before you know it, the player is unsettled and more often than not, the information they've been given is probably wrong anyway. Their current club might see their star asset's form dip and ultimately, they are the losers in this whether they get a decent transfer fee or not.

Despite all of the above, football is the only profession I know where you can't approach an employer and ask if there's any chance of a job – freedom of movement should be allowed in my opinion. Contracts for players in football work pretty well, but that's not the case for managers which are an absolute waste of feckin' time – and I speak from experience with this. A manager's contract, in reality, is only as long as the good form of his team because if you lose six games in a row, most managers will be sacked, so you could say – in effect – you've never really got a contract that's more than six games long!

It's just naive to think tapping up doesn't go on all the time and on one occasion, I witnessed a former player – shall we say, 'encouraging' – two of my lads to move on at our own training ground.

There were strong rumours a former Rovers player was on the verge of signing for a new club, so I called him up and asked if he wanted to come back. I knew full well I couldn't match the wage other clubs were offering him but hoped the success he'd enjoyed with us previously might just swing it.

We had to at least match the £200,000 offer because our fans wouldn't have been too happy if we'd not even made the effort to bring him back. As it was, in his infinite wisdom he chose to go to a different club, but he would further piss me off no end with something he did after signing for them.

I arrived for training one day to find this player in our training ground kit room talking to two of our current strikers. I said to him, 'What are you doing here? Get out you stinking shit-head pig! You're not welcome round here anymore.' He started laughing because he thought I was joking, but I wasn't. I was majorly pissed off at him – even more so when I later found out he'd been telling them how much money he was on at the other club – just maybe in an attempt to get them to join him?

Whether that was his idea or somebody else's, I'll never know – all I know is he made it perfectly clear he was on considerably more than they were at Rovers. Unbelievable! As I say, I know it happens all the time and players talk amongst each other regularly, comparing wages and bonuses, but to come into my own backyard and do it was totally disrespectful to me and Bristol Rovers FC.

I couldn't believe that he actually had the balls to come to my training ground to seek out two of my best players to tell them they were on rubbish money. From that day on, I think both players lost a little bit of their focus. Something changed. It was hard for them when they were playing at the top of their game and were being paid what they were. Then, when somebody who isn't playing anywhere near as well as they were signs for your neighbours and gets three times as much, you're not going to put up with it for very long, are you?

Agents have to earn their money somehow, so they stir the pot all day, every day. And that's just the way it is.

There was a time I was in administration at QPR, Chris Wright was the chairman but Nick Blackburn, his right-hand man, was the acting chairman and I was told I couldn't buy any new players because we had no money. Nick told me if we brought anyone in, it had to be for free.

So I spoke to this agent (who I won't name) about buying a player (who again I won't name) on a free transfer. We chatted about his wages and came to an unofficial agreement and then he said, 'OK, onto agent fees. How much do you want?'

I said, 'I beg your pardon? I was led to believe there was no transfer fee involved.'

The agent said, 'Well there's no transfer fee as such, but you can go back and tell your chairman the cost will be £50k to get the deal done and we can divvy that up between us.'

I asked him what part of our discussion he had misunderstood? I was fuming – as I was a lot during my time at QPR over one thing or another – and said, 'Listen, I don't take money off my football club to bring a player on a free transfer and we've got no feckin' money anyway. You're not getting paid for this so why are you talking about money? You said he was a free transfer; I'm interested in taking him, but free transfer means free!'

Ha! How does a free transfer cost fifty grand?

I spoke with Nick Blackburn later that evening and told him exactly what had been said and he said, 'Thanks for telling me,' and we did get the player eventually; he didn't cost us anything and the agent got nothing. That was the only time in my career I was offered what is commonly known as a 'bung'.

I remember Arsene Wenger once telling me they were signing this French lad and he had six 'representatives' all in the room saying, 'I did this for him' or 'I did that for him' and the kid, who'd come from the ghettos and looked totally perplexed, said, 'Can you pay them all? I owe them all something' because each had claimed to have helped him at some stage of his career. Now they all wanted to cash their chips in and dip their beaks. Imagine that? Christ. It's ridiculous and there's no sport quite like football when it comes to hangers on, parasites and freeloaders.

BEST SIGNING(S)

WHAT a question to be asked! I've had so many great signings that it is almost impossible to pick them all out, but what I will do is go for a couple of players I signed at the start of my managerial career because if I hadn't got them right, I wouldn't be here managing still in 2025, would I?

The two biggest risks I ever took were when I bought a couple of lads from non-League football. Both were quite valuable assets to their clubs, so we weren't talking about paying peanuts for them. The first was Barry Hayles who was playing for Stevenage at the time and when I first went in for him around 1996, he broke his leg and was ruled out for a year. I knew the lad had something special, so we waited and went back in for him 12 months later. We had to pay what I felt was an awful lot of money to get him – £400,000 – for a player just coming back from a serious injury and at 26, was not a kid. It was a huge risk, but thankfully, he was fantastic for us and 18 months later we sold him to Fulham for £2million, so don't you just love it when a plan comes together?

Deals like that win the confidence of the board and the trust that came from that one deal was priceless and that's why Barry Hayles was one of my best ever signings as a manager.

Another lad we took from non-League that went on to earn

Rovers a sizeable profit was Nathan Ellington. He was 17 at the time, so everything could have totally gone wrong, but we paid Walton & Hersham £150,000 and after a couple of years, we sold him to Wigan Athletic for £1.6m so Nathan would have to be up there as well. Both were considered pretty costly gambles by Rovers' standards because they were unproven at League level, but both turned out to be fantastic players, great lads and wonderful investments for Bristol Rovers. People look down their nose sometimes at non-League footballers sometimes, but I know from experience that there are a lot of uncut diamonds out there if you are prepared to give them a chance.

TAKING A
'GAP YEAR'

WHAT do I think about the so-called 'gardening leave'? Not that much and my garden never improved during the time I was supposed to be tending it. Sometimes, you find yourself between two jobs with your hands (sometimes) contractually tied, and I'll always think of the time between leaving Leicester City in 2008 and becoming Blackpool manager in 2009 as my 'gap year'! It was a kind of crash course in DIY, making bespoke chicken coops, media work, watching games and a hundred other things I did while I worked out which direction I was heading for.

I felt jaded and totally drained after the Leicester City experience – a bit like Austin Powers when he had his mojo extracted. I think I'd fallen out of love with football for the first time in my life and I needed to step back for a while and take stock of my life and career. I still looked for work and just a week after leaving Leicester I was invited for an interview with Scottish Premier League club Hearts, but I didn't have my UEFA A badge at that point, so they didn't follow up their interest, even though I was starting my course a week later.

I was totally pissed off with the system and how it was held against me because I quite fancied a spell in Scotland, so I called up Sir Trevor Brooking at the FA and was a bit angry with him, almost shouting at him at one point but just stopping short, thank goodness. Imagine anyone being angry at Sir Trevor? I was angry and frustrated, and I'd probably brought a lot of it on myself by saying what I'd said while I was at Plymouth – all of which I'd meant, but then I chose to move to Leicester where pretty much everything went wrong. There are times when you think you can do this or that and feel like you're invincible, but really you are anything but – you're just as vulnerable in football as you are anywhere else.

I was on something of a learning curve and several weeks later had an interview for the Huddersfield Town job. I spoke with one of their old managers, Stan Ternent, and he said I should definitely speak up if I wasn't happy about anything they said during the interview, so I did – and I never got invited back!

I went in there warning the chairman that he'd had a lot of managers in a relatively short space of time and one bloke had been a common denominator throughout that period – Gerry Murphy – and I said, 'Are you sure you've got him right?' I never heard from them again. Murphy had been caretaker-manager three times, and I was led to believe he had almost as much influence as the manager. So it probably wasn't a good move to go in and tell the chairman his go-to guy might be a problem, especially if he liked him so much!

It makes me wonder how much, subconsciously, I actually wanted that job at that particular moment in time. Even as Kim and I drove towards Huddersfield we were asking each other whether we really wanted to live there and the honest truth was we didn't, so I can't say I shed too many tears about not getting the job. I must admit, I did think my past experience and reputation might actually get me the position, but it didn't and the same happened when I went in for the Swindon Town job, which put me in a difficult situation at one point – one I wouldn't like to be involved with again.

Kim suggested we go and take in a game and the nearest one to us that weekend, which ironically was between two managerless sides – Swindon Town and Huddersfield Town. We were going to see some of Kim's family who lived just up the road from the County Ground, and it seemed like a good idea just to get back into watching games again. Both teams were struggling but, perhaps a little naively, I didn't expect what happened that day to happen.

I went into a pub at the back of the ground and chatted with a few people who came up to say hello before we left for the match. As we walked across the car park, a reporter put a notepad under my nose and said, 'I hear you've been saying you'll have the job within two weeks.' I got a bit lairy and asked him which job, as well as enquiring as to what he was on about. It was a bit weird and at half-time, Swindon were 2-0 down, some of their fans must have spotted me in their end and started singing my name. I was completely embarrassed by it all and so I left, realising I couldn't go to a match anymore unless I had a reason to be there. People were adding two and two and getting 156.

I did eventually apply for the post at Swindon, but I didn't even get into the last four! I again had gone to the interview, been honest with the chairman and board and told them the direction I'd need to move in if I got the job – but obviously it wasn't what they wanted to hear and they looked for somebody else. I think you either suit people and a club or you don't, and this was another case of me not being right for that particular club. Thankfully, 16 years later they finally came around!

The scary thing was starting to think about the possibility I might have to consider doing something else for a living. I'd been in football all my life but despite all my experience as a player and a manager, I concluded that none of that was much use in the outside world. I couldn't adapt managing a team into any other walk of life because the job is a specialised area of employment, isolated from most other work. I was thinking, 'what if no other chairman – ever – likes the way I talk? Can I change my outlook or way of expressing my concerns in order to find a job? There are 92 chances to manage a League team in this country and I'd already used up four of those with Plymouth, Leicester, Swindon and Huddersfield.

We were renting a house near Bristol and were in a kind of limbo – I had no job, we were living on farmer's land and the money I'd been paid off with from Leicester was dwindling away fast. That massive severance we managers get as mentioned earlier in the book! I'm not one of these managers who gets millions of pounds as a pay-off – it doesn't work like that at my level. I was looking after my family, paying rent, renovating my house in Plymouth so we could let it out to students and there was a time when I wondered if anybody would want me as their manager ever again. I think people looked at me and thought, 'Oh, there's Ian Holloway. He'll be alright because he's done this and that and is in the limelight' but the truth is I was just the same as anyone else. Nobody asks your opinion when you're out of work, the world sort of forgets about you. Football, I believe, is something where you almost have to start from scratch every day.

I started doing all kinds of things including making chicken houses for the hens we'd bought and did a bloody good job, even if I do say so myself. *Soccer AM* came down to the house to mock up an advert about my bespoke chicken coops and made up a load of jokes about it that were quite funny in a way. I did think I'd get one or two orders from football supporters around the country, but there wasn't one single taker because they probably just thought it was a wind-up – what other football managers sells chicken coops for feck's sake?

After that, however, I started working on the radio for the BBC and did some TV work for Sky. I really enjoyed the radio work, I have to say. It was nice being sat high up in the stand chatting to people, giving my opinions on tactics and suchlike with no pressure at all. I just said things as I saw them, did it my own way and thoroughly enjoyed myself and got great feedback, too. It was also good to be watching football again on a regular basis and, more importantly, to have a reason to be there other than leaning on someone's shoulder thinking, 'Christ, I could do with your job'. It made me care about football again and it was hilarious to mix with both sets of fans and hear what they had to say.

I was working for BBC Radio 5 Live and having a ball – it all felt right, and I did a few Friday night shows, putting a manager's slant on various discussions. And because of the new connections I'd made, I was given two tickets to the Champions League quarter-final between Chelsea and Liverpool in April 2009. I'd always promised to take Kim to a top match one day, so we decided to make a night of it. We stopped off at a bar in Knightsbridge and got chatting to some Liverpool fans and by the time we left, I was adorned with LFC badges – I was in the Chelsea end, so I took them off before I went in so's not to get filled in and then sat down to watch one of the greatest games I think I've ever seen.

We saw the whole range of emotions football supporters can

go through that night in a magnificent 4-4 draw. It could have gone either way with both sets of fans up one minute, down the next and to hear some of things that were being said at different moments during the game up close was enlightening. As we left the ground I said to Kim, 'Please don't ever let me listen to what another supporter thinks' because I'd seen them boasting, panicking, boasting, panicking before ultimately being relieved. It was an education that I felt privileged to have witnessed and I vowed to take all the additional knowledge I'd learned back into football with me.

Mixing with the fans and commentating on games from the stands made me realise that this game is all about entertainment. I think it's really important to tell supporters exactly why I make certain decisions and get my message across clearly. I've realised a lot of choices I was making during certain points of my managerial career were because I was acting on raw emotion like the supporters do and I couldn't do that again. I sat down and thought about all the things I'd learned during my year out of football and how I would handle things if I got another crack at management, though I wondered if that chance would ever arise, having been turned down by a couple of lower league clubs.

Our home life began to settle down after Kim and I found the perfect home to renovate near Bath, with enough land for my family and our chickens, when out of the blue I got a call from my agent saying Blackpool were interested in talking to me. Almost a year to the day since I'd been sacked by Leicester, I was back in the game...

MIND GAMES

MIND games. They say Sir Alex Ferguson was the master of this dark art and who could forget Kevin Keegan's rant as Newcastle United manager when Sir Alex managed to get inside his head in the race for the 1995/96 Premier League title? But what about mind games that can actually benefit a player – one who is struggling to find their form because of things they couldn't control?

New signing Jason Roberts was having a hard time settling in at Bristol Rovers and had only scored once in 14 games for us after signing in 1998. Gary Penrice was one of my striker coaches and he had sussed out what he thought the problem with Jason was, which I believe sums up what Pen is all about. It was annoying Pen because he felt Jason could do a hell of a lot better. He came up to me one day after training had ended and said, 'You've got to come out with me this afternoon, Ol, because I've realised what I've got to do with this kid. He's potentially got what it takes, but if I can't get him to focus, he's never going to be the striker we want him to be.'

I told him no problem, and he added that it wasn't going to be very pleasant. I said I didn't want to know what he had in mind, and he should just go ahead and do it.

'I've got to do it, Ol' he insisted – 'and I want you to witness it.'

So we took out a few balls, along with our goalie, Andy Collett, who didn't get along too well with Jason anyway and was very chirpy and self-opinionated. It turned out to be one of the most inspired sessions I've ever taken part in.

And Pen began. As we stopped in front of a goal, he said to Jason, 'Your trouble is you can't focus, son and you're letting everyone and everything get inside your head.'

Then Andy Collett piped up, 'Yeah, that's right. I'll save whatever you've got.' Jason wasn't having any of it and wanted to turn around and go back in but I told him it's OK and not to worry. I started laying the ball off to him and he was hitting shots all over the place.

Pen, stood behind the goal, shouted, 'Oh, you can focus then, can you? That's shit, absolutely useless.' Jason soon lost his temper and I was starting to wonder if this exercise was going to work when Pen called a halt to the session. He came up to Jason and said, 'I'm telling you now you've got no focus. Your technique is fine, but you just can't concentrate, you let your mind wander and I'm going to prove it. I'm going to shout some things at you and if you're as focused as you claim to be, you'll put most of the balls in the back of the net.'

We began again and Pen stood behind the goal again and began as I started laying the ball off for Jason. He shouted, 'You're useless Roberts, you fucking tosser!' Jason continued to shank his shots wide and Pen told him not to listen to him and ignore everything he was saying. 'What a feckin' waste of money! I was out with your mum last weekend, Robbo.'

Eventually he managed to block him out and he started channelling anger and frustration and started scoring, and scoring, and scoring. 'Go on, that's it,' said Pen. 'Get your head over it, well done, that's it – now that's focused, son!'

By the end of the session, Jason was invigorated and looked

a changed kid. From that moment on, he believed in himself again. The difference in him from that day forward was nothing short of amazing, and it was all down to Pen's expertise. As far as I'm concerned, it was also the mark of his genius because I don't believe there are many around like him. And it was such a simple session that he did, in reality.

I recalled Jason to the starting line-up for the FA Cup first round tie with Welling a few days later and he scored all our goals in a 3-0 win. He then scored in a 1-1 draw at Millwall and got another in the next game at home to Oldham. He'd end the season with 23 goals from 37 starts – not bad for a player who'd got one in 14 before that. Proof, perhaps, that sometimes mind games can be a very positive way of getting into somebody's head.

HOUSE RENOVATING

BUYING a beaten-up old property because it has potential had its pitfalls, as Kim and I discovered back in 1987. And even to this day, we haven't learned our lesson because as I write, we're doing something similar today! Back in 1987, I had just signed for Rovers after a nightmare stay with Wimbledon and we had moved in with Kim's folks and stored the furniture in her dad's garage while we looked for a new home.

Within a few weeks we'd found a lovely old house in need of renovation – most definitely a 'fixer-upper' – and I came up with a hair-brained scheme to do the work myself. I took my dad around and he absolutely slaughtered it. 'What are you doing you idiot? What are you thinking about? This is a hell of a job, and you've got no chance of getting this into shape…' He went on for a bit, but we bought it anyway. I think he could see it was going to be a bit of a money pit, but we had envisaged what it could be like, and with a baby on the way, we were determined to get a big family home ready for the winter.

With the help of my mate Paul Lewton, who was a worka-holic builder, we reckoned we could just about do it. I'd been

IAN HOLLOWAY

away once and come back to Bristol and I couldn't ever see
myself leaving again, so we put our heart and soul into the
renovation work. On my afternoons off, Kim and I would nip
off to Bath and browse antique markets and bric-a-brac shops
looking for knick-knacks, fittings and furniture.

Dad would come around and give me a hand from time to
time, but he wasn't well and was getting chest pains – probably
much more severe than he let on. Kim used to despair when
Gary Penrice would turn up unannounced and take one look
at me covered from head to toe in dust and say, 'Coming out
for a game of golf, Ollie?' He hadn't changed a bit, though in
truth, after my experiences at Wimbledon, it was good to see
him again. Kim would invariably tell Pen I was busy – in so
many words – and on one particular day I told him I had to get
on with painting the skirting boards.

The next day at training, I walked in, and all the lads were
on their hands and knees painting imaginary skirting boards
around the dressing room. Pen was a bloody nightmare but
because he was a fully qualified plumber and could have helped
me out, I called him up and told him I needed a plumber
urgently and he said, 'No problem, mate, just look in the
Yellow Pages under 'P',' he laughed at his own joke and then
hung up. Like I said – a bloody nightmare. Who needs mates
like that?

I was always in a rush to get things finished and on one
occasion I almost paid the price for my haste. I was doing some
tiling and had to take the light switch off, but didn't turn the
mains off first. As I was doing the last few tiles I touched a live
wire and shocked myself. I couldn't get away from the bugger
and as the doorbell rang, I somehow managed to fall backwards
onto the floor with my hair stuck out. With a distinct smell of
singed flesh and hair in the air, Dad walked in the room and

shook his head. 'I shall have to live until I'm 150 to look after you, you silly sod.'

I'm amazed I'm still here to tell the story and my advice for any young couple thinking of doing the same? Buy a new build!

BAD LOSERS

ALL managers are bad losers – it's a fact of life and probably an obvious statement, but none of us want to lose... ever. Maybe some accept a loss better than others and maybe some don't lose very often and so it's easier to be gracious when that is the case.

The pressure is constantly on and as I've said before, managers only seem to be as good as their last result.

The person I'd say was the worst loser is Neil Warnock. He had a way about him that was so competitive he'd drive you insane but now I know him better, I get what he was trying to do.

Neil had a knowledge of the referees because he is a qualified official, so he was always moaning at them and in the fourth official's ear.

Steve Evans is another manager who is perhaps misunderstood because of how he is when the game is going on – so both Steve and Neil are ultra-competitive and sore losers – but they'd probably both say I was worse than they are! And they might have a point!

We've all seen the video of Neil getting stuck into his players, but that comes from frustration and a deep-rooted attitude of 'I don't ever want to lose' that he probably has more than anyone I've ever met.

We did have a big barney once when he accused me of doing what he does all the time – influencing the referee. I told him it takes one to know one and added that I didn't have a clue what he was on about because I was shouting at the ref because I thought he was wrong. I said, 'I'm not trying to influence him, Neil, but because you know the rules, you try and do that all the time!'

I added, 'I've got a grievance with him which I'm allowed to air, why don't you mind your own feckin' business?'

I said I would never try to influence a referee because I'd call that cheating and he said, 'Oh, so you're calling me a cheat?'

I said, 'Yeah, I am. And I never really enjoyed that people called you Colin Wanker (an anagram of Neil's name), but you really are what people call you.'

After that we got on fine because things like that don't stick. I got to know him better after that and understand what he was doing and why.

I was once on the end of a Mick McCarthy tongue-lashing as well. I picked a Blackpool team that was perceived as weakened when we played Aston Villa away and we got beat – I got fined £25,000 for that – and I argued in a press conference that Mick had done something similar. Afterwards he called me up and said, 'What are you dragging me into it for you fucking pillock? I thought you were my mate?'

I told Mick I was and that I was just trying to explain it wasn't fair and he said, 'Well don't throw me under the fucking bus!'

I'm sure Sir Alex was as bad, but I don't know him as well. I only saw him with a face like thunder on one occasion after the QPR side I was part of had beaten United 4-1 at Old Trafford and I am just glad I wasn't in his dressing room that day. Seriously!

I've seen Pep, Arteta and Jurgen Klopp get angry and usually that's with officials – we don't usually lose it with each other unless you are Alan Pardew and Arsene Wenger. And if we do exchange words, it's usually over in a flash and we shake hands at the end.

It's normally the referees who get the blame rather than blaming ourselves or our teams. You have to own what you say and sometimes that isn't easy.

JAMIE CARRAGHER

I SAW the video of him spitting towards that young girl and I must admit it was pretty gross. But I don't know enough about him to really make a judgement other than when he was a player when he was a class act – both him and Steve Gerrard – in the way they led Liverpool by example. Each time my Blackpool team beat them, they were the first to congratulate us. And they meant it.

That incident was a horrendous moment that I don't know the whole story of, but I'm certain he quickly became aware of how much he'd let himself down and his family. I believe he apologised for his actions.

People are capable of goading footballers, managers, celebrities or whatever – I would never spit at anyone, but there have been times it's made me angry. I suppose we all need to question how we would react in certain situations.

I was coming out of Swindon after a game recently and a woman said as I passed, 'That Kabongo Tshimanga – he ignored me last week.'

I said, 'No, he wouldn't do that.'

She insisted he had and so I said, 'Are you talking about him over there?'

She said, 'Yeah, that's him. He ignored me last week.'

I said, 'Well maybe if you get his name right it would help – that's Tunmise Sobowale, not Tshimanga, so you're blaming totally the wrong person there. And I said Tshimanga wouldn't do that, so don't say that's him when it's a totally different person.'

She said she was ever so sorry and I said, 'Well tell him – and don't shout him back because it's not very polite is it? I'd run and catch up with him.'

Kim and I were once called 'Cadbury c**ts'. I'd just been presented with my Bristol Rovers lifetime badge and as we left a Rovers fan shouted that at me and Kim. I'd gone back to my old club to be abused. The woman in question was pissed out of her head and then walked into a car before her other half led her away.

You just have no idea what's going to happen, do you?

I don't mind banter with people, but I don't get spiteful with people or hold it against them, and I think that goes back to my dad's advice all those years ago telling me to make sure I didn't take myself too seriously.

If somebody is unbelievably abusive to you right to your face, what do you do? Pretend you haven't heard it? That would be a very difficult thing to do, I can tell you. Just because you are well-known, it doesn't make you public property.

So, spitting was a terrible reaction – he was forgiven by his employers, he realised he'd made a terrible misjudgement and apologised for his actions. Case closed.

HYPOCHONDRIA

DOES it exist in football? Are there hypochondriacs out there? My god, yes there are.

Sometimes the pressure gets too much for some individuals, and they get injury after injury – now, is that because they are genuinely injured, or is it because they are making a meal out of it?

If I see any of my lads in the physio room, I always say to them, 'You're one of three things – sick, lame or lazy – which one is it?' And I might add that they could be a hypochondriac!

I remember when I was managing Bristol Rovers and Pen – Gary Penrice – was going through a horrible spell when he wasn't scoring, and then he broke his leg. Kim said he actually looked relieved! He'd been going through such a lean spell that suddenly that pressure had been relieved.

But then, if the team does well in your absence, that creates its own pressure because you're not sure if you're going to get back in the side again.

Injuries can have a psychological effect on players, too. If you suffer a seemingly innocuous injury that turns out to be serious, it can really affect the confidence you have in your own body. You lose belief in yourself, and you can almost distrust your own body and your physical mechanisms. You can over-worry and err continually on the side of caution because you aren't 100% sure that you are not going to break down again.

Ironically, one of the fittest players I ever had was one of those I almost never had available – or at least that's how it felt. Marc Nygaard was a strapping 26-year-old we signed at QPR from Brescia. He did a mile-run drill the best I'd ever seen anyone do it in 2:57 minutes and looked as though he was jogging. But I could barely get him fit after that because he was like a racehorse – he was so finely tuned. He was absolutely ripped, and you could see his veins on his muscles, but he would never play through a niggle. Most of the time, we always have something that is causing a slight issue, but when Marc had that – which was most of the time – he flatly refused to play. He'd say, 'No, that will go if I do that' or words to that effect and he ended up no use to me whatsoever. He played 69 times in about three seasons, so you'd guess he was – on average – out for 25 games a season during his time at Loftus Road.

In fairness, he'd suffered an ACL injury when he was around 22 and some players are never the same after that. Marc was chiselled out of granite – but unfortunately he wasn't made of it, and it was such a shame because to look at him, you'd have thought he was the perfect physical specimen.

Injuries are the worst part of football because of the physical and mental toll it can have. You are suspended in time and in some ways you have to go backwards while your body repairs itself and while it does, you don't know if you are going to be the same player you were before. It's hard enough to get into a professional XI at the best of times, let alone when you've had a bad injury, and you are working your way back.

The hypochondria theory you might harbour about a player

can, however, occasionally backfire on you. I had a player called Arthur Gnohere who I swore was playing a sick card on me – I was convinced he was making it up. I called his bluff and told our medical team to send him for a scan which cost us a fortune. The scan revealed he needed a feckin' operation! If I'd kept my mouth shut, he'd have probably just got over the issue and it might have repaired itself. You have to be careful with how you handle these things as I discovered to my cost.

To summarise, in my experience, the players under the most pressure seem to pick up injuries more than the others – particularly centre-forwards who aren't scoring! We do everything we can as clubs to help players physically, but I don't think we do enough to help them mentally. Hypochondria is a mental issue caused by worry and I always try to support my players. I know I might have had a bit of fun with some of the stories above, but I'm well aware that it can be a serious problem and that's where football should really come into its own.

WORST INJURIES

INJURIES are a nightmare, and I feel for players who genuinely suffer bad ones. In February 2025 my Swindon team were taking on Chesterfield and I saw one of the worst injuries of my career when their defender Tyrone Williams went down after a collision and the lad couldn't feel his left arm or left leg. It was awful and I just hope the lad goes on to make a full recovery because at the time of writing, he'd just undergone surgery and things looked very serious.

And who could forget that horrific injury Coventry's David Busst suffered away to Manchester United in 1996 when the lad's bone was showing after breaking his leg? That ended his career there and then – you just never know what's going to happen when you cross that line to play football.

Without doubt the ones that immediately concern everyone are the times when a player just literally drops. Christian Eriksen has made an incredible recovery after he collapsed on the pitch playing for Denmark, and we also had Fabrice Muamba for Bolton Wanderers and more recently Tom Lockyer at Luton. And nobody will ever forget Marc Vivien Foe's tragic death playing for Cameroon in Lyon.

I have a lad at Swindon who has had to have a pacemaker fitted to regulate the speed of his heart – Nnamdi Ofoborh who

288

was with Steven Gerrard at Glasgow Rangers before he joined us. We're trying to get Nnamdi going again as he learns to deal with his heart going slower and he's been out for the best part of four years. But I think he's going to be great for us.

Injuries are part and parcel of football and if I ever have an owner ask me, 'Why's he not playing? Why am I paying him so much and he's out all the time?', I'll just say that it's their fault for buying a football club because injuries will always happen.

GROUNDSMEN

GROUNDSMEN are a fantastic breed – the best in the world – and every one of them is a character.

Jackie Pitt was the groundsman at Bristol Rovers, and he was an absolute legend. He'd been a wing-half for Rovers and played about 500 games – he was small, but wiry and aggressive – and he eventually became the club's groundsman. If you dared go anywhere near his beloved playing surface, he'd try and kill you.

He had guns everywhere for shooting any pigeon that went near his grass seed, and I'd never seen anything like it. I came in one morning and he was dressed head to toe in camouflage gear – I said, 'What the hell are you doing?'

He said. 'They're after my seeds – I'm going to get every one of the bastards!'

I asked him what he was on about and he said, 'Come on, I'll fucking show you!'

We went to the side of the pitch, and he told me to crouch down. He lay at the side of me, blending in with the grass in his army gear, and he started to pick them off one by one. He was a hell of a good shot, too. It was horrible because he'd hang the dead pigeons up around the ground to try and discourage the others like some ancient black magic warning. He was crazy but everyone loved him.

Groundsmen are so protective of their playing surface – it's like their little baby – and every one of them I've met over the years has not been quite right if you get my meaning. The pride they have is quite sensational but look at the surfaces they provide these days compared to the ones I used to play on in my day. They put in such care and effort and the hours they invest is incredible.

When they tell you to 'get off my pitch'. What do they mean? Players are going to run around on it, do sliding tackles, cut it up and perform knee slides on it if they score a goal. They're actually providing a service so we can do all the above, so why are they telling us to get off it? Ha!

QPR's playing surface wasn't that good when I first arrived as a player. They had three patches that got uber damp – a bit like quicksand or running through a bog. The lads who played a lot knew it, plus where to avoid if possible and they warned me about it.

In one of my first games, I went to close a player down on the wing and looked easily the favourite to get there first, but I slipped in the bog, my feet got away from me and so did the player. The fans were going mental at me because I must have looked so slow. So I don't miss the days of erratic, unpredictable surfaces one bit.

In the end, QPR replaced it with a new £600,000 playing surface. The difference was like night and day – you went from having twisted ankles and muscle strains due to slipping and sliding to blisters all year around because the ground was now so hard.

We are getting a new £150,000 pitch at Swindon this summer – the first time it's been re-laid for nearly 20 years!

NERVIEST MOMENT

THIS was at Blackpool in May 2010. It was between us and Swansea City who got the final Championship play-off spot. We were at home to Bristol City and were drawing 1-1, but Swansea were also at home to Doncaster Rovers and also drawing 0-0. If Swansea scored, they would go above us and those last few minutes, not being able to see what Swansea were doing as we waited for the final whistle was just excruciating. Then we heard our fans cheering – it was because a Swansea goal had been disallowed – and I could see my lads thinking it was all over at Swansea and that we'd done it. I had to shout, 'For feck's sake get on with it! They're still playing!'

We managed to hold out and so did Doncaster so we went into the play-offs, beat Nottingham Forest home and away and then came twice came from behind to beat Cardiff City 3-2 at Wembley and go up to the Premier League. But my question is – how come it was Bristol City we had to face that day? Of all the clubs! Those buggers have plagued my life! And how can my 1,000th game as a manager be against Grimsby Town, where I'm not the most popular? Come on! It had to be them or Millwall didn't it? And how can I take Blackpool to the Etihad, batter Man City who were joint top of the table, and my half-time sub Matt Phillips gets the man of the match award... when we lost 1-0? How can that be? The Football Gods... they like a good laugh, especially when it's at my feckin' expense!

THE EX-FACTOR

HOW often in football does a former player of your club come back to haunt you? I'd go as far as saying the stats would be unusually high and it's become a staple of my management career that I try to actively use those sort of things to my team's advantage. As I write, in the past few weeks two of my lads have played against clubs they were once with. One scored two against his old employers and the other got a penalty a week or so later – I'd actually recalled him to the starting line-up exactly because of that added 'ex-factor', so it definitely works! They have an extra bit of zest and purpose to do well and prove maybe either the manager or the fans wrong, so it gives them a boost, an additional edge. If you can use that team's advantage, sometimes it can make all the difference.

In fact, it's probably one of the main reasons when you're loaning a player that you have to make a gentleman's agreement not to play the player against his parent club. And to underline that, the only time I can remember that not happening was when I was at Blackpool. I borrowed Marcel Seip from Plymouth Argyle, and I said to their chairman that I would only take him if he was allowed to play against Plymouth or else I'd sign somebody else. They agreed he could, and he scored on his debut against them in a 2-0 win! Marcel was seeing the Plymouth chairman's daughter at the time, and he was seen celebrating our goal, which didn't go down too well with the Green Army!

One thing I'm happy to say I never did was play against Bristol Rovers in my whole career. If I had, I'd have wanted to win because I'd want to beat my granddaughter at tiddlywinks if I could.

MOST MEMORABLE MOMENT

THERE'S been a lot of these, so I've had to think long and hard about it – and what I've come up with is the luckiest and unluckiest moments in my career so far – both of which happened at the same time.

I'd been playing on loan for Torquay United in the Fourth Division and it looked like we were going to go out of the league in a horrible, unforgiving relegation battle. I was on loan at Plainmoor and returned to Brentford, but I kept up with the lads at Torquay and was hoping and praying they would stay up.

On the final day, Torquay were playing against Crewe Alexandra knowing that if Lincoln City and Burnley bettered their result, they would become the first team to be automatically relegated out of the league.

Crewe were safe and relaxed and went in at the break leading 2-0. That meant Torquay were bottom of the table as things stood. They pulled a goal back – and here's the lucky and unlucky bit – when there was a bit of a commotion in the corner of the stand, the police went over to sort it out as emotions were obviously running high.

At that same moment, Torquay's Jim McNichol collected a pass down the wing and was running towards the corner where the trouble had been. One of the police dogs – Bryn – thought Jim was about to attack his handler and so sank his teeth into his leg as he drew closer. As the medics treated Jim and the handler removed Bryn's teeth from his leg, the game was suspended.

About 10 minutes added time needed to be played, by which time the other games that day had finished. Burnley had won, but Lincoln had been beaten 2-0 at Swansea, so Torquay now knew exactly what they needed to do. And that was to score a goal – which incredibly they got deep into additional time to make it 2-2 and get the point they needed to send Lincoln City down.

What are the odds of that happening? So, it might have been a game I wasn't playing in, but I was fully invested in it and you can see the good luck was the dog bite and the bad luck was also the dog bite! Good old Bryn – he's a legend to this day among Torquay United fans. One of those incredible stories you only get in football – there's nothing like it.

I could talk forever about some of the things I've seen because we're the modern gladiators – thumbs up or thumbs down – because you've got to please the mob, but I'm not sure you can ever really do that. Being part of it is a privilege. Trying to lift your lads up and make them believe again when they've just lost or keeping their feet on the ground when they've just won. Trying to make a player better than they ever believed they could be… my god, what a challenge and we are playing a game that is more complicated than chess because you can never truly control it.

That ball is continually on the move and even if you are the best coach in the world, you can't control what the opposition are doing. How is that possible? Manage the game? Good luck with that! You can only adjust.

Football is the greatest learning tool. It can heal a wound and do everything all in one go and thank god I liked it as a kid because it's given me nothing but joy. And after four years away, I couldn't be happier to be back in among all the madness.

ACKNOWLEDGEMENTS

FIRST off, as always, I'd like to thank my wife, Kim, for all her love and support over the years, and for giving me my beautiful children, William, Chloe, Eve and Harriet.

To the scout who first found me, Joe Davis and coaches Bobby Campbell, Bobby Jones, Colin Dobson and Bill Dodgin Sr, for my early grounding at Bristol Rovers and the great and much-missed Gordon Bennett, my first mentor.

To all the friends I've met or played alongside during my career – you all know who you are – thanks for everything. My dad told me I'd meet some wonderful people in football, and he was right.

And I'd like to thank my old mate Gary Penrice for writing the foreword. Pen's knowledge and friendship has been a constant in my life for 50 years and his judgement of players is second to none.

Also, the guys at Reach for giving me the platform to share my thoughts in this book – a football book that I wanted to be a bit different.

So thanks to Chris Brereton for commissioning the project, Clare Fitzsimons for continuing Chris' great work and Simon Monk for the brilliant editing. Also thanks to Chris Collins for the wonderful cover design.

Finally, I've left this bit until last on purpose because without these two I wouldn't be here in the first place – my mum and dad – Jean and Bill Holloway, who have always been my inspiration, then and even more so today.

Ian Holloway,
February 2025